Myths for the Masses

An Essay on Mass Communication

Hanno Hardt

Blackwell
Publishing

© 2004 by Hanno Hardt

350 Main Street, Malden, MA 02148-5020, USA
108 Cowley Road, Oxford OX4 1JF, UK
550 Swanston Street, Carlton, Victoria 3053, Australia

The right of Hanno Hardt to be identified as the Author of this Work has been asserted in accordance with the UK Copyright, Designs, and Patents Act 1988.

First published 2004 by Blackwell Publishing Ltd

Library of Congress Cataloging-in-Publication Data

Hardt, Hanno.
Myths for the masses : an essay on mass communication / Hanno Hardt.
p. cm. – (Blackwell manifestos)
Includes bibliographical references and index.
ISBN 0-631-23621-X (hardcover : alk. paper) – ISBN 0-631-23622-8
(pbk. : alk. paper)
1. Mass media – Social aspects. 2. Mass media – Political aspects.
3. Communication – Social aspects. I. Title. II. Series.

HM1201.H37 2004
302.23 – dc22
2003023165

A catalogue record for this title is available from the British Library.

Set in 11.5 on 13.5 pt Bembo
by SNP Best-set Typesetter Ltd., Hong Kong
Printed and bound in the United Kingdom
by TJ International Ltd., Padstow, Cornwall

For further information on
Blackwell Publishing, visit our website:
http://www.blackwellpublishing.com

for Slavko Splichal

Contents

Preface

This two-part essay is a reminder of the importance of historically grounded debates about language, theories of knowledge, and communication that have occupied European thinkers since the Sophists began to teach the art of persuasion by eloquent speech and Plato observed that communication between individuals is only possible when a common ground exists for meanings or ideas. The following discussion is informed by a critical intellectual tradition in Western thought that identifies the idea of mass communication with power relations and hegemonic struggles, but also with collective cultural practices and individual empowerment over time.

Recent considerations of mass communication and culture or society are only the latest extension of sentiments regarding meaning, power, and effect. They are embedded in social and political skepticism, and a mistrust of the possibility of absolute knowledge. The latter characterized Sophist attitudes and informs contemporary thought: from doubts about a universal truth – spread by Friedrich Nietzsche and Sigmund Freud, for instance, and responded to by Jacques Lacan, beyond the tradition of rationality, objectivity, and truth redefined in the early works of John Dewey, as well as by the more recent contributions of Michel Foucault – to an experience of reality through language and writing that relies on notions of human agency and self-determination.

The idea of mass communication is significantly affected by these theoretical considerations, from its incorporation into the realm of

The media of public communication . . . constantly profess their adherence to the individual's ultimate value and his inalienable freedom, but they tend to forswear such values by fettering the individual to prescribed attitudes, thoughts, and buying habits.

Max Horkheimer, 1941

cultural practices, as in the work of Raymond Williams or Stuart Hall, to the crisis of representation and production, as noted by Jean Baudrillard and Umberto Eco, among others. A postmodern view of mass communication, in particular, contains the destabilized hierarchies of fact/fiction, objectivity/subjectivity, and truth/falsehood; it introduces a process of de-differentiation and leaves individuals to deal with the consequences of facing multiple meanings, knowledges, and truths.

The essay draws on these challenges to the popular, historical knowledge of mass communication to address the specter of an ideologically constructed media reality, which defines democratic institutions, and whose impact on the lifeworld of the social self is based on the construction of myths by the dominant economic and political order. Such a media reality, to paraphrase Ernst Cassirer, is given to us at the outset in definite forms of pure expression that flow from the presence of mass communication in everyday life. The essay is thematically organized to address the relations of mass communication to self and society, respectively. To increase readability and to aid the flow of ideas, traditional notes and references have been dispensed with in favor of short quotes or paraphrased material; the curious reader is referred to the bibliography for the work of the respective authors.

Book projects are never just solitary intellectual ventures, but rely on the efforts of many individuals. I wish to thank Jayne Fargnoli of Blackwell's, who suggested this project, for the opportunity to formally consider the working reality of mass communication, and Janet Moth for her expert editorial assistance. I benefited from the critical readings of earlier drafts by Bonnie Brennen, Ed McLuskie, Peter Robinson, and Vida Zei as well as from the detailed comments of one anonymous reviewer. And I am grateful to the Faculty of Social Sciences at the University of Ljubljana (Slovenia) for its continuing support of my work.

Hanno Hardt
Ljubljana/Iowa City
November 2003

1

Mass Communication and the Promise of Democracy

Mass communication is a primary force in the determination of society, while the principle of mass production and consumption remains an essential and prevailing influence on its deployment. Mass communication defines democracy and helps mold the social character of the modern individual as a predictable, if not anticipated, participant in the discourse of a capitalist society. Institutions of mass communication – since their earliest incarnation in Western civilization – are the defining channels of the cultural, political, and economic discourse of society. Their articulations shape the image of other social institutions and give them meaning; they also help construct ways of seeing individuals as masses. Indeed, contemporary society is unthinkable without the overwhelming presence of the media, while the never-ending process of mass communication generates a working reality that defines relations among people and events. Both mass communication as a socially determinant and politically significant process of meaning-making and its increasingly powerful institutional presence in society constitute a major challenge to understanding democracy in terms of individual participation in the process of communication. Therefore, serious understanding of the significance of mass communication in contemporary circumstances must begin with a critical examination of its social, political, or economic foundations and the cultural construction of its place in society with the goal of accommodating a search for a more inclusive (or more democratic) social order. After all, Hannah Arendt reminds us that the word "social" originally means an alliance of people for specific, political, purposes. Integrating mass communication into democratic practice is a culturally specific and intensely social project with political overtones.

I

It is a commonplace that mass communication is currently in crisis, since profits are down and public confidence in the media remains low. It is less of a commonplace, however, to argue that this crisis may have its roots in a failing dialectic between communication and mass communication that distinguishes the public discourse of the twentieth century and ultimately determines the quality of being in the world. More precisely, the dualism of experience and learning – the first product of understanding and the process of coming to know, according to Immanuel Kant and John Dewey, respectively – has been seriously challenged. While mass communication as a determinant of social and political realities has multiplied experiences of the world – or increased empirical knowledge – it has failed to equip individuals with an intellectual disposition – or rational knowledge – to competently approach the complexity of the world with confidence.

The revolutionary shift from communication to mass communication – which had begun with the increasing mobility of the text and the invention of the printing press – finally overturned a delicate balance between the authenticity of individual expression and the inauthenticity of institutionally manufactured articulations of reality in the twentieth century. Consequently, while mass communication as a media practice contains political and economic priorities that redefine its traditional role in a democratic society, as an idea it conceals a flawed conception of a democratic way of life with an increasing isolation of the individual by private (economic) media interests. As Max Horkheimer observed over 60 years ago, the media profess to adhere to the values and freedom of the individual, but they "fetter the individual" to prescribed thoughts, attitudes, and buying habits instead. Indeed, the intellectual paradox, recognized early on by Horkheimer and Theodor Adorno,

2

appears in the effects of media fare that produces a manageable or controllable social formation.

The current practice of mass communication confirms the dominance of a private, commercial agenda in a democratic culture that has failed to deliver on the promise of participation, which seemed to have been intended when mass communication – in the language of the confident middle class – stood for liberation and represented the road to enlightenment and freedom. In the meantime, the media do not belong to the people, yet people need media for access to knowledge about themselves and the world, while the media must deliver audiences to meet commercial demands for a functioning regime of consumption.

Moreover, since media have replaced "the other" in a historical process of alienation and isolation that characterizes industrialization, the new relationship is shaped by the commercialization of mass communication. Consequently, individuals discover their selves in a process of consumption that matches the expectations of a mass-mediated reality rather than in conversations with the other. Furthermore, the process of communication itself is being undermined with the introduction of virtual realities, for instance, in which individuals are isolated from others and converse with themselves.

And yet, the rise of mass communication is also tied to a realization of the centrality of communication in social settings and the extension of media practices that affect private and public behavior; it prospers with the growth of literacy and the spread of universal education, and bursts forth as a way of life with the popularity of mass-mediated experiences as a modern alternative to self-expression. Consequently, mass communication is the discourse of society, which defines, organizes, and determines life in its social or political manifestations.

Mass communication was also instrumental in the twentieth-century crusade of modernity, where it remained a key element in the unfolding of the future. It reveals a philosophy of change in action that promises enlightenment while pushing at the boundaries of the imagination of a captive public. Mass communication rises to become an irreplaceable cultural representation of the age.

3

Because of its significance in the creation of the contemporary lifeworld itself, the process of mass communication deserves close scrutiny. Its uses in the name of liberty and democracy, its identification with ideologically driven campaigns – such as the push for a free flow of ideas – or its role in the determination of social or political truths, disclose the nature of society. These applications have notable consequences for the collective responses of people, since public knowledge relies exclusively on media productions of reality – or, as Niklas Luhmann reminds us, whatever we know, we know through media.

Mass communication and the world of the media are by tradition tied in Western societies to the rhetoric of democracy. The term democracy is difficult to define, however, since its use is not only politically and emotionally charged, but also claimed by ideologically diverse contenders for an alliance with the principles of a democratic life. Its basic premise, popular self-government, is augmented by conditions of universal suffrage, political liberties, and the rule of law. The American version involves the safeguarding (and balancing) of individual and group interests, including issues of assembly, expression, and publication. Thus, the guarantees of freedom of speech and press relate the functioning of democracy to the performance of (mass) communication. Besides, insistence upon unfettered communication becomes the operating condition for a democratic system of government. A malfunctioning of this process, caused, for instance, by political or economic interests – and involving issues of power and authority, among others – must endanger and ultimately destroy the possibilities for a democratic way of life.

Appeals to protect and reinforce democratic principles rely on a linkage between democracy and mass communication that has traditionally been located in the idea of community and its principles of equality, participation, and communication; these principles constitute the dynamic and determinant elements of success or failure of mass communication practices in the spirit of a democratic society.

The process of mass communication itself has acquired credibility with its traditional claim that the media serve the public interest and, unlike other cultural institutions, deserve legal protection. Based on the premise that individual rights and freedoms also belong to corporations as legal persons, the result offers extraordinary protection to commercial interests, which are charged with acting in a socially responsible way under the protective cover of the constitution. In fact, over the years, a socially and politically motivated protection of mass communication (or free speech) – per tradition – has become the responsibility of economic interests, which have used the process of mass communication to construct a market-oriented version of democracy in action. As commercial interests in mass communication have become stronger and more pervasive throughout modern society, political authority has been absorbed by economic power. Under an ideological and institutional umbrella of democratic conventions, mass communication has been reconfigured to respond to commercial concerns in ways in which economic capital helps shape and reinforce the social and political will of society – all the while being strengthened by enormous profit margins, especially during the latter part of the twentieth century. In other words, capitalism prevails under the guarantees of the state, or, as Fernand Braudel once observed, capitalism only triumphs when identified with the state, indeed, when it is the state.

As a result, the mass production of information and entertainment – supported by an authoritative, economic interest in public responses to commercial or political appeals throughout most of the last century – has steadily eroded the give and take of participatory communication. Indeed, the past century is marked by an increasingly complex and desperate struggle between individuals and institutions over social, political, and economic forms of existence on the territory of communication. Who speaks, where and when, and under what social or political constraints, have become important questions, since an individual shouting into the wind or the specter of town-hall meetings are no match for sophisticated technologies of mass communication.

Even access to the means of mass communication, such as local cable television, broadcasting, or print journalism, is insufficient to offset the relentless pursuit of centralized, institutional media power that has affected the realm of personal and social communication and shapes the imagery of a world outside individual experiences. As a result of these developments, mediated realities have given rise to a new understanding of fact and truth, reshape the premise of social knowledge, and redefine personal interests.

Consequently, participation is configured as authentication of the dominant agendas of consumption in a world that engages industrial means of mass persuasion to create self-serving realities and efficiently replaces what one remembers of John Dewey's democratic vision of communication with references to communities of compliance or consumption. The idea of sharing – which defines the sensibility of community and perfects the practice of communication – re-enters the public sphere as manufactured consent and commodity exchange that reflect the interests of those in control of the marketplace of ideas. In other words, the notion of sharing turns into a process of investing labor and capital in economic propositions with social and political consequences that benefit commercial interests.

At stake is the commercialization of human relations with the assistance of mass communication. Since reality is always what people think it is, the reality of contemporary life emerges from an immersion in the social or cultural practices of mass communication that are tinged by commercial claims or political goals. Ways of thinking, speaking, or seeing among individuals are the outcome of a permanent exposure to a discourse of power in the public sphere. Moreover, there is no social or political life – or meaningful social practice – outside a mediated reality, which is not the result of institutional strategies of convergence.

Henceforth, the idea of mass communication reflects the properties of mass society in its totalitarian excesses, and guides considerations of culture and society that have serious consequences for an understanding of the self and relations with others in the world. What is rarely comprehended is the historical role of commercial interests in the construction of social realities, including the reality of a democratic life, in support of a specific *Weltanschauung*. Such constructions are accompanied by the fading chance of recovering the self in communication with others and of re-establishing a sense of mass communication as a dynamic process that caters to the public interest.

What emerges from these introductory observations is the realization that mass communication is a politicized process – involved in consensus-building or in what Antonio Gramsci calls an expansive hegemony – which serves the dominant ideology. At the same time, as long as the idea of democracy retains its provisional quality of being the unfinished business of the people – and of being open to change by definition – the idea of mass communication remains equally responsive to the will of people and their struggle for change. After all, the development of modern media is closely related to the historical struggle for freedom and democracy.

II

The history of mass communication (and its definition) materialized over several centuries from a chronicle of shifting power, when preoccupations with control over nature are accompanied, if not replaced, by desires to dominate individuals (or societies) through persuasion and manipulation. It is also reflected in the turn of science from astronomy to sociology and psychology, when language and communication became the territory for human inquiry. This territory expanded with the rapidly improving sophistication of communication technologies – especially during the twentieth century – to perfect the process of mass communication. Deeply embedded in the cultural fabric of contemporary society, mass communication defines reality and marks the boundaries of social knowledge, authenticating its representations of the world through public compliance and consent, if not sheer popularity.

Mass communication is the originator of a public discourse that changed from social initiatives to institutional domination. It borrows from the notion of communication, however, which arises from reflections about the self, community, and the prospects of democracy. "Communication" refers to a basic human condition, recognized much earlier in Western philosophical works and articulated in the context of social and political thought throughout Western history, with a contemporary meaning that harks back to the fifteenth century. Referring to the process of "making common," the term has been applied (as a noun) to a wide variety of practices that establish commonality, from road- or waterways, and telegraph and telephone connections to institutional forms of

7

communication and human dialog. Since its meaning includes significantly different practices, including the notions of "transmission"
(one-way) and "sharing" (two-way) — as well as the middle ground
of "making common" — the use of "communication" requires a
more specific reference to its intended application.

The term "mass communication," on the other hand, has its
ideational roots in the evolution of societal communication in
Western cultures. Its long and distinguished history runs parallel to
the expansion of publicly shared information after the increasing use
of papyrus facilitated the dissemination of private and public records,
when scrolls circulated throughout the Mediterranean region, for
example, and the Roman "acta diurna" — usually accepted as the
first prototype of the newspaper — provide a source of information
about daily events never seen before 131 B.C. Paper-making
processes from China supplanted papyrus by the twelfth century,
when paper mills developed throughout Europe. Block prints pre-
ceded printing, as demand for copies of written tracts had also
increased throughout Asia, until movable type had appeared in
China, Korea, and Japan by the eleventh century — about four centuries before this process emerged in Europe. Gutenberg's subsequent invention became a turning point during the Renaissance
period with the liberation of the text from the manuscript age.
Indeed, the sixteenth century saw the production and dissemination
of multiple copies throughout many regions of Europe and beyond
at moderate prices, accompanied by an increasing pace of social,
cultural, and political expansion.

But the circulation of knowledge and the public use and
exchange of information would become regular features of a social
existence only with the arrival of broadsheets after 1400 — and
newssheets printed from type after 1456 — which initiated access to
ideas and availability of information to the public at large. From
1609, newspapers (*Zeitungen* in German; *nouvelles* in French) began
to appear across Europe; it was not until 1690, however, that
Benjamin Harris succeeded, with Boston's *Publick Occurrences, Both
Foreign and Domestick*, in launching a newspaper outside of Europe.

The rise of the press (and the printed word) was accompanied
by the increasing prominence of the image as a tool of persuasion,
but also as a subject of theories of knowledge that focus on image

8

and imagination; the latter was initially conceived as an intermediary between perception and thought. Images became representations of reality and, once passed through the mind, passed for reality. The use of images soon became popular among politicians and others, and not only for pedagogical reasons. In comprehending images one "adheres to" what they represent, including the intent with which they have been fashioned, according to Christian Jouhaud. This process made the image a powerful tool of persuasion, recognized long before its modern versions – in the form of photography, film, and television – rekindled the debate.

The beginning of the eighteenth century marked a turn to the modern phase of mass communication. It proceeded from an already sophisticated understanding of the indispensable presence of newspapers in politics and in an "orderly" world, according to Kaspar Stieler's remarkable observations in 1695. His comments about the benefits of news are based on an expectation of truthful reporting and its potential for enlightenment. His analysis also reflects a sophisticated approach to what was then a revolutionary media technology only a few years after the introduction of the printing press in central Europe. There was an anticipated purpose to the organization and operation of the press that foreshadows much later hopes for a democratic model of mass communication. Since then, an increasingly literate public has become more and more reliant on the process of mass communication – that is, on the production and dissemination of knowledge (through books and pamphlets) and information (or news) by journalists with expertise in manufacturing items of interest for the enlightenment of a general public.

Of course, the concept of mass communication took a more clearly defined shape during subsequent centuries: which experienced an improvement in communication technologies until the end of the nineteenth century, when new media systems entered the public arena to serve the specific needs of an industrialized, urban society. McLuhan's observation that every medium shapes and controls the conditions of human association and action confirms a technological determinism that yields fashionably narrow explanations at the expense of a much broader cultural perspective on the relations of technology and society, however.

At the same time, still and moving images began to encroach on earlier meanings of mass communication, to move social communication more consciously beyond pure language to imagery, while the rise of broadcasting implied a return to the spoken word and introduced sound as an environment for information and entertainment. The aural experience defined the uses of radio within private or public spaces, and its later portability produced a moveable technology that liberated the listener from the confinement of place and time. The result was not only the availability of new and different media – beyond painting and printmaking – with their commercial potential (from photography, film, and television to radio), but a heightened sense of mediation, or of recording and transmitting information linked to the production of aural and visual realities.

Also, the possibility of reproducing the world "as it is" with the aid of photography – and later film – for instance, created a rivalry with the word that has lasted until now, although the initial fear that the word would be replaced by the image did not materialize in the twentieth century. Photographs introduced a new language of mass communication which transcended the written or spoken word; they offered illustration and explanation of nature and humanity. Photographic images dwell on the fact and promote a positivistic view of the world that appeals to readers, who value the immediacy of the object and cherish the reality of the image. The picture advanced as a means of social and scientific identification, or proof, and became a reliable language of mass communication, embedded in the context of words, and read with confidence by those looking for empirical truths. Indeed, pictures confirmed a believe in the objectivity of mass communication (journalism) and contributed to its credibility. Later on, television would build its reputation on the strength of the image in the discourse of society.

Today images determine this discourse of society with their presence (or availability) across a range of media. They help construct reality and impose views or perspectives that conform to ideologically determined expectations. Baudrillard argues that they bear no relation to any reality and are their own "pure simulacrum." In this case, images are the new vocabulary of a postmodern capitalist society, in which the individual is dazzled by the spectacle – and misled. In fact, Guy Debord's "society of the spectacle" provides a theoretical context for a culture of consumption from which mass communication emerges as both process and outcome of a conversion, which replaces the object with an image that becomes reality and message simultaneously.

The discourse of reproduction at the center of mass communication, which materializes in the practice of representation, is also characterized by the inauthenticity of the process. For instance, the technical progress of the means of mass communication reduces distances between cultural producers and their audiences by producing encounters that fake a comfortable proximity between the consciousness of alienation and the experience of participation. But mass communication cannot solve basic human problems and merely reflects and solidifies the ambiguities of media-controlled forms of social and political authority. The possibilities of the self and the discovery of an authentic discourse remain hidden beyond the articulations of mass communication.

By the 1920s mass communication had become a worldwide phenomenon that helped create the contemporary face of a global environment. Pictures and sound became the ultimate building blocks of a mass-mediated reality that would shape the social and political landscape of modern societies. Their presence gives realism a place in the arsenal of mass communication strategies to gain credibility with representations of the "real" world. Beginning in the 1980s, the internet responded to the need to reach beyond the effectiveness of mass mediation. It drew large numbers of people into a web of commercial activities of global proportions by appealing to individual initiative and freedom of choice. This is not a mass communication "revolution," however, like the invention of the printing press, or the birth of a visual culture, which privileges the eye, as when photography and film came into societal use early in the twentieth century. Rather, it extends the availability of information, or data, to individuals with interests and capabilities to conduct independent research and draw their own conclusions.

In the meantime, the continuing growth of society – in the United States and elsewhere – had popularized the idea of "mass society" as a descriptive characteristic of processes of industrialization, urbanization, and modernization, which increasingly modified

11

the social order as social control became centralized in bureaucratic practices. The latter, however, contained the possibility of breeding totalitarian tendencies to contaminate democratically conceived institutions of public communication, for instance – and in the presence of effective totalitarian regimes elsewhere. Edward Shils once observed that the availability of mass media is an invitation to their demagogic use. Especially after 1945 – with lessons learned from Nazi propaganda campaigns – individuals became susceptible to mobilization and control through mass communication, as the new sense of being was increasingly defined in terms of alienation, anonymity, or mobility. It was a time when "mass culture," characterized by the "mass production" of standardized products for "mass markets," appropriated the process of "mass communication" in a general trend of massification – which actually began centuries ago with the operation of the printing press.

These terms locate the idea of mass communication in a capitalist society under conditions of centralization and mass production, which include not only products but also consumers or audiences. At a time when the notion of "mass" indicated conditions of change, characterizing social or political movements or activities of societies – from socialism or capitalism to scales of production and consumption with their respective ideological implications – the term mass communication acquired its social scientific meaning of serving large numbers of people. Indeed, it was the movement of information to pander to large and diverse audiences that was to distinguish mass communication from earlier forms of social communication, when publics were not considered markets and appeared less heterogeneous and less dispersed. In addition, mass communication implies a one-way process of communication that reinforces the power of media institutions – or of those who own or control them – to set agendas for a society which relies increasingly on fewer sources of mediation for more of its social knowledge.

The latter development contains the potential for totalitarian practices – identified by specific visions of mass society – which threaten democratic notions of communication based on freedom and individualism, and assign the phenomenon of mass communication to general processes of mass society. References to "mass" –

which began with Herbert Blumer's recognition (in 1939) of a new type of social formation, beyond group, crowd, or public – for example, also lend a specific character to the manner of communication, to the way of reaching large numbers of individuals, or to the character of the audience itself.

More specifically, mass movements of modern times – if one thinks of fascism, communism, or Nazism, in particular – have sought total political control over society with the help of intellectual elites and their expertise and access to mass communication. Contemporary pluralist societies also manage the masses – sometimes identified as assemblies of unqualified individuals – with the aid of mass communication produced by an expert minority. In either case, elites organize and determine the nature of society, introduce their renditions of democracy and its practices, and reproduce their versions of reality with the help of mass communication. Indeed, mass communication and the notion of the masses are interdependent ways of denying individual autonomy through strategies of separating people from themselves.

What differentiates totalitarian from democratic uses of mass communication is the degree of participation and access to the means of mass communication available to the general public, as well as the degree of freedom of speech and press that accompanies mass communication practices. Unless, that is, we have reached a point – as Albert Camus once feared – where such a freedom either depends exclusively on the power of government or the power of money.

There is a curious connection between the rise of mass communication – which incorporates the historical growth of media industries – and the emergence of the totalitarian properties of mass society in the conduct of a democratically conceived process of mass communication. Thus, an increasingly atomized society conceives of producing communication practices that create a pseudo-pluralism of voices in pseudo-communities with mass communication processes that are centrally determined and, therefore, jeopardize the workings of a participatory democracy.

Mass communication in capitalist societies is the voice of a corporate age, which simulates the presence of communal ties and the possibility of shared experiences for the masses. More likely, however, is the general practice of subjugating individual interests, cultural preferences, or ideological differences to a leveling process that encourages consensus and guarantees compliance among large numbers of individuals. While mass communication may originally have been conceived by society as a way of gathering, producing, and disseminating information (or sharing entertainment) – and in this sense as a communal activity – it has subsequently been appropriated for private profit or political control, suggesting a significant change in the nature of earlier understandings of mass communication. In either case, mass communication appears as a force for integration, positively through assimilation into a common culture and negatively through hegemonic practices of incorporation.

The emerging definition of mass communication, then, extends beyond traditional considerations, which have been inspired by a social scientific focus on the objective properties of mass communication without addressing the historical conditions of societal communication that have ultimately resulted in alienating and anti-democratic practices.

A clue to an understanding of the complex, economic nature of mass communication – which invites extrapolation – has been offered by George Gerbner's definition, in particular, of mass communication as an institutionally based mass production and distribution of a broadly shared, continuous flow of public messages. He outlines social and economic determinants, which demand a more complex review of the process of mass communication, without referring directly to its ideological nature, however. The cultural, social, and political components of mass communication constitute a complex process that is institutionalized in media practices.

In a context of technological processes in modern society, mass communication represents the systematic application of specialized knowledge for the purposes of producing (or reproducing) knowledge and information efficiently; indeed, mass communication as technology projects an environment for creative labor, and in its institutionalized form becomes a constitutive force in society. Its instrumentality produces the conditions under which human communication occurs, including the reduction of dialogical relations, for instance, and the privileging of media at the expense of conversation.

Thus, the definition of mass communication as technology focuses on the process of rationalization – the effective transfer of social communication into the realm of mass media – and the effects of individuation – the fragmentation of traditional communities that comes with the isolation of the individual as reader, viewer, or listener in the system of mass communication. At the same time, media technology represents a set of societal norms whose effectiveness depends on the degree of internalization of the idea of mass communication in a particular cultural setting.

The term "mass communication" itself was allegedly coined by Harold Lasswell in the early 1940s in the context of government work related to propaganda activities during World War II. Since then, the nature and function of mass communication has occupied US social sciences as a process and in the context of a larger progressive agenda regarding the nature of democracy and the need for social control in a society of immigrants. Mass communication – unlike the concept of mass society – had not been considered an ideological construct, involving the construction of audiences, communication experiences, and communicators, as well as availability, cost efficiency, and appeal to the masses in a larger, political sense. But its impact on society, although contested in its details, became a foregone conclusion, backed by an age-old belief in the persuasive power of the (printed) word and confirmed by the increasingly technological sophistication of the means of communication; they enjoy a widespread reception as powerful sources of persuasion.

An appropriate functional description of the process, according to Wilbur Schramm, an early promoter of mass communication as an academic discipline, is mass communication "acting as society communicating," which involves institutional sources (media) and destinations (individuals or groups in society) as well as effects, or the specific uses made of messages. It is an approach to a definition that has dominated traditional media research with an emphasis on the large-scale, one-directional, and asymmetrical nature of mass communication as a social process.

Subsequent definitions, however, remain decontextualized and ahistorical statements of the roles or functions of mass communication; they are not the result of a genealogy of communication as a cultural (or historical) phenomenon with specific roots in a

15

concrete historical moment and with a definite presence among real power relations in society. Indeed, these characteristics are well described by Robert Merton's distinction between a (European) sociology of knowledge and an (American) sociology of mass communications. The latter concentrates on mass phenomena, such as popular culture and opinion-making, and develops analytical tools to examine information rather than knowledge in society's pursuit of immediate results.

More recently, the term mass communication has been revised by a cultural analysis of contemporary society, initially under the influence of Raymond Williams, who argues that there are only ways of seeing people as masses. Consequently, the idea of mass communication is an expression of this conception and a commentary on its function, which inspires talk of massification, breeds disharmony or animosity, and poses a danger to democracy. Williams liberates the individual from the ideological trap of a "mass" society and restores the values of a common, participatory culture with a more workable concept, like communication.

Beyond Williams, the field of cultural studies has incorporated the notions of communication into a much broader, interdisciplinary consideration of culture and cultural production by theorizing beyond the level of message construction and circulation and by contextualizing the idea of communication historically and ideologically. Also, cultural studies is less interested in broad, institutional perspectives – such as relations between mass communication and democracy, for instance – but more in basic, emancipatory practices of individuals related to issues of meaning-making, social or political power, and human agency in the process of communication.

In a more general sense, the idea of mass communication translates into a reification of communication in all of its physical and ideological manifestations – aural and visual, free and controlled – through a process of industrialization and within a system of material and intellectual cultures that is fully developed in industrial societies. The result is a commodity form that satisfies some human wants and has the power of exchangeability. Since mass communication streams relentlessly into the consciousness of individuals to dominate representations of the modern world, its constant presence raises questions about the most rational – that is, accountable and regulated – control over mass communication to secure a democratic existence.

Finally, there is the notion of defining by doing, which introduces a personal dimension to a search for meanings of mass communication that escapes any institutionally grounded, historical claim to a definition, since it is identified with particular choices of respective users. What emerges from such an approach is a litany of individual preferences that range from bourgeois self-interest in perpetuating or preserving specific social or political conditions to the interests of the oppressed or marginalized, whose own choices vary with the details of their oppositional stance.

In any case, these defining instances of media functions also include the creative applications by a public who may be more interested in background noise, moving color images, or wrapping-paper – among other self-defined objectives – than in the actual reception of information or entertainment, for instance. Although far removed from any original intent of their producers, these media uses do occur, and their histories need to be written for cultural balance in traditional versions of mass communication history which typically celebrate the process of production rather than the manner of consumption and, thus, favor an institutional rather than an individual biography.

III

Indeed, while mass communication figures prominently in the history of cultural evolution and social advancement, it is not entirely a story of betterment or progress, nor is it one in which progress is an entirely Western achievement. Instead, it is the story of a universal struggle, in which communication in its technical manifestation is the outcome of creative labor in many parts of the world, albeit more often than not for similar purposes of social or political control through propaganda and advertising.

The emergence of mass communication from the depths of fifteenth-century Europe was a slow and deliberate process – after the success of the printing press, the advancement of postal services, the rise of literacy, and the spread of knowledge through universities and academies of science. There was also a new curiosity about the world, which promoted travel and encouraged journalism. Together, these developments signal the beginning of rationalization and commercialization, based on the powerful if not persuasive merger of capital and technology, which brought about a shift in thinking about production and consumption. These signs of progress were accompanied over time by critical analyses of contemporaries such as Comte, Marx, and Weber, among others, who focus on the process of centralization and the forging of modern societies at the expense of individual existence and cultural integrity. In fact, the centralization of power, accomplished by the annihilation of space and time, has always relied on the available means of communication – including transportation. There has been, then, since the earliest times, a conspiracy of ideological power and technological speed, which has helped determine the contemporary role of mass communication in the expansion and reinforcement of political or economic authority.

More specifically, the struggle for freedom of the press, and the protection of ideas circulating in books or pamphlets, were part of a struggle for the liberation of bourgeois claims amidst the transition from feudal to capitalist societies. Mass communication was instrumental in the growth of a bourgeois society with the liberating potential of education. At the same time, mass communication served political and economic goals to control and direct the fate of society. In either case, its working context was culture, in which mass communication helped reproduce the desire for freedom and happiness (*promesse de bonheur*) through cultural outlets ranging from poetry and fiction to philosophical tracts and political treatises.

The rise of a modern civilization with the presence of pamphlets, books, and newspapers, for instance, revealed itself with the passage of a class society into the industrial age. The unfolding of a cultural history in Western societies begins with European elites, their acquisition of intellectual tastes and articulation of class standards, and ends with universal education and widespread access to the stream of mass communication, initially provided by journalism and liter-

ature. Implicit in the course of these events is the changing relationship between the production and circulation of social knowledge from hierarchical to democratic structures controlled, however,
by commercial interests.

Thus, the bourgeois control of mass communication, which historically had rested on a privilege, needed defending against fading
aristocratic claims on power, on the one hand, and against a growing
rebellion from below, on the other, since literacy provides not only
access for the masses, but, equally important, access to the bourgeoisie. Indeed, the democratic practice of sharing information in
the twentieth century retained some forms of a privileged, class-
related enterprise that took advantage of its access to the needs and
desires of people as subjects, who, in turn, adopted bourgeois behavior and tastes in an effort to rise above their social standing. The
promise of a middle-class existence, involving the potential of literacy and the propositions of mass communication, became the major
attraction of the American way of life.

With these developments also came significant attitude changes
towards the written word as a source of power, followed by a fundamental challenge to the cultural and political status quo. After all,
language as an external manifestation of thought acquired stability
with the new prospects of the text that began with the manuscript
age. Writing as a new technology – which remains a more revolutionary invention than printing many centuries later – would
become invaluable for purposes of learning and the rise of literature. In fact, Mirabeau once noted that writing and money are the
two greatest inventions, since they produce the common languages
of intelligence and self-interest. Both inventions were soon to be
combined with the rapid commercialization of mass communication. Writing preserves not only the discourse of a culture, but gives
shape and substance to the physical and psychological manifestations
of contemporary life. It also reinforces the original bond between
language, myth, and religion and is a reminder of the mythical
power of the word as a primary force in society, not unlike the
power of money as a movable symbol of economic value. Money,
on the other hand, preserves power over the means of mass communication and ensures control over the form and content of the
discourse. It is also a basic form of a commercial language, which

19

– according to Georg Simmel – expresses qualitative differences of objects in terms of "how much?"

The idea of empowerment through words has always encouraged scholarship in linguistics, from ancient Greece, when philosophical thought passed from nature to language, to the nineteenth century, when language with a particular reference to cultural history became a reflection of the history of peoples, and to the twentieth century, when sociological considerations characterized everyday language as a system of communication. Language, in other words, is recognized as a fundamental, highly charged cultural medium. In fact, it is the center of a culture.

Since all cultural products are language-embedded, they are texts open to interpretation. Recently, language has been intimately connected to culture through explorations of meaning and meaning-making, a territory for observations regarding individual empowerment and the role of the media in the discourse of society. Language allows individuals to name things and make them present in their minds; it is a constitutive element of social identity; language also continues to be appropriated by mass communication to augment comprehension, ensure compliance, and secure conformity. In this context, language use is an ideological practice that reflects knowledge, beliefs, attitudes, and relevant social or political constraints as it delivers the power of naming to mass communication for its representations of the world.

Writing as a technology, capable of circulating ideas in time and space, permits cultural or political indoctrination with the help of an increasingly sophisticated media technology. But even in its most advanced forms of persuasion – for example in advertising and propaganda – mass communication still relies on the mythical force of the word to gain influence through strategies that are based on the use of language. In fact, language becomes the source of commodification, when meanings are subverted as styles are created and circulated to fit market demands.

The use of propaganda (or persuasion) is as old as the need for social control and has accompanied human history from ancient promoters of war or peace to modern strategists of conflict resolution. Propaganda is an institutional activity in the hands of governments, political parties, and religious or private organizations; it relies on confidence in the use of symbols, ranging, for instance, from the emotional appeal of the national flag or the holy cross to expressions of motherhood or friendship, couched in terms suitable for mass communication.

Since ancient times, the circulation of information has played a major role in the realm of religious indoctrination, for instance, when Catholicism seized upon opportunities for spreading papal policies and the word of God throughout its empire. In fact, Christian theologians have always been particularly interested also in the use of imagery as an effective means of instruction and conversion that would supplant the word among illiterates and – in a more sophisticated and symbolic form – encourage contemplation among the learned few. Hence, mass communication was applied by the church – which remained the main source of propaganda (or persuasion), and the great enforcer of the word, continuously until the eighteenth century. When democratic principles entered public life, however, those who had gained political and economic (or military) power insisted on secular allegiance to the state.

The rise of nationalism – frequently intertwined with the growth of capitalism – heightened demands for throwing off the domination of the church. A literate public became a potential threat to the social order, and traditional authority, like religion, sought new institutional mechanisms to absorb and organize class and community. Thus, Protestantism made use of the support of printers (as intellectual workers) and their religious agitation, for example, to help advance the cause of the Reformation through mass communication.

As secular institutions developed, government by consent required indoctrination of the governed into the social, political, and cultural fundamentals of a democratic existence. The press played an increasingly important role in the education of an informed electorate. For instance, Thomas Jefferson not only believed that education and schooling would produce an enlightened electorate, capable of participation in the political process, but he also appreciated the presence of the press for the protection of democratic practices and the unrestricted dissemination of information and opinions.

With the Industrial Revolution, political and commercial propaganda represented daily encounters with ideological campaigns to change traditional norms of society, while avoiding conflict and assimilating the masses through various forms of persuasion. Edward Bernays, who had grasped the power of mass communication and its potential uses for purposes of change, and who knew that human nature is susceptible to modification, also confirmed the view that society is dominated in politics or business by a few individuals who understand the "mental processes of the masses."

Mass persuasion utilizes any form of social myth or popular culture for circulation by various social institutions, from newspapers and magazines to education. In modern times, state propaganda has become an organized effort to indoctrinate society and to ward off the adversarial endeavors of mass persuasion. Thus, large-scale political persuasion came of age during World War I in the United States, where George Creel, who had roused Americans to religious fervor against Germany, considered his work the "world's greatest adventure in advertising." His activities not only disclosed the consequences of government propaganda, but revealed the possibilities of manipulation through mass communication. Although social scientists agreed by the late 1930s that propaganda had only limited effects, Americans remained wary, when the threat of World War II called for renewed government propaganda. Indeed, Harold Laswell, who saw propaganda as a management of collective attitudes through manipulation of significant symbols, characterized it in 1927 as a "new dynamic of society." His observation continues to reverberate with the contemporary activities of public relations and advertising in politics and commerce. The idea that persuasive power could be an important weapon ultimately shifted to the field of psychological warfare and carried propagandists beyond World War II.

Although the institutional framework for government propaganda was dismantled after the war, the idea of propagandizing society for purposes of ideological warfare – against communism, for instance, or terrorism, for that matter – resurfaced as various government agencies began to employ public relations as a legitimate means of informing their respective publics. The realization that mass communication was vital to the success of creating and sustaining world views that serve government policies was a powerful incentive to convert public media, such as the press or broadcasting, into major carriers of official information. Consequently, privately owned media organizations continued to help legitimize government pronouncements regarding the state of the nation or the state of foreign affairs. Their coverage, more often than not, exhausted itself in the mere reproduction of ideologically determined government information. This practice accommodated bureaucratic goals but violated journalistic standards of maintaining professional skepticism regarding government pronouncements.

Advertising, like propaganda, is the art of wrapping the truth in imagination, as has been suggested. But while propaganda is often subtle, couched in half-truths, and packaged as legitimate information or news through public relations efforts, advertising, which shares some of these characteristics, is ubiquitous and inescapable in modern times. It appears directly, marked by its place or time in the stream of mass communication, or indirectly, hidden in the narratives of journalism or fiction, but always tuned in to the rhetoric of mass society. In fact, advertising is the twentieth-century literature of the masses and a source of their social knowledge. They cling to it with suspicion, but also with no real alternative, because advertising is accessible, brief, and repetitive, produced in the language of an industrial society in which real people in real-life situations are doing real things as they relate to each other. Advertising also reinforces the myths (of freedom and equality, among others) on which society relies to illustrate its understanding of democracy.

For these reasons, advertising messages appeal to people who like a story, crave a positive outcome or happy end, and continue to participate in the process of mass communication, as long as the payoff is a good feeling, satisfaction without guilt, or just the thought of belonging. People react to commercial messages irrespective of the real conditions of existence, the prevalence of false needs – whose content and function are determined elsewhere – or the lack of autonomy. The encounter with advertising also reveals the use of familiar sounds or visions of mass society, which discovers itself buying its own experience and contributing unwittingly to its own seduction.

Thus, advertising furnishes material goods with social meanings in response to expressed or anticipated false or true needs. The former are those which perpetuate toil, misery, and injustice, according to Herbert Marcuse, while the latter are those of vital interest, such as food, clothing, and shelter. Indeed, advertising encourages waste and hastens obsolescence by identifying products with personal aspirations; obsolescence also works against the quality of products and, ultimately, against the quality of work.

Advertising is also a pursuit of realism as a form of expression and, therefore, a search for a universal language – like photography or visual imagery, for instance – to help shape the process of mass communication and to maximize desired responses. In its ever-present manifestations – which interrupt print narratives, cut through the flow of aural or visual information, or dissect the cityscape – advertising creates a two-dimensional reality, in which familiar dichotomies (such as new/old, improved/not improved, extra/normal) mark the boundaries of consumer choice. In doing so, advertising reveals the contrast between the complex, destabilizing conditions of a contemporary existence and the mythology of an easy life between two options with a highly predictable outcome.

The choice, however, becomes problematic when expectations of a manufactured consumer reality turn into real demands for a better existence. Even worse, the result is frustration among those addicted to a make-believe world of advertising, who may well be aware of the differences between their own economic or social reality and the fiction of advertising, but refuse to abandon the myth of consumption as redemption, which is reinforced by a constant and repetitive stream of mass communication. Indeed, mass communication and advertising are technically and economically merged, as Max Horkeimer and Theodor Adorno conclude after considering the pervasiveness of advertising in 1940s America. They see advertising and mass communication join in the mechanical repetition of consumer products and call advertising a negative principle and a blocking device, because whatever does not bear its stamp is economically suspect.

This intimate relationship between advertising and American culture is founded on the commercialization of mass communication, which began during the nineteenth century as a formless, irresponsible, and unregulated activity. Samuel Hopkins Adams wrote in 1909 that advertising has a thousand principles, one purpose, and no morals, and a contemporary that to discover the truth of an

advertisement it is necessary to "read between the lies." But advertising matured rapidly to become a formidable business with an
almost unlimited potential as commerce and industry expanded, and
there were new markets to be conquered. During the 1920s advertising recovered from public criticism and converged with culture
to reflect the American way of life; it became increasingly difficult
to distinguish between reality and pure advertising imagery.

Over the next 80 years, the growing volume of advertising revenues created not only wealth for the media industry, but also a
growing dependence on these profits for the survival and well-being
of media organizations. Today advertising serves economic interests
and reorganizes the flow of mass communication, as, for example,
in the segmentation of information and entertainment in broadcast
media by commercials. In other media, commercial interference
ranges from the harmonious use of color in print media, or the
interaction between editorial copy and advertisements, to visual and
aural styles drawn from other materials to obscure the boundaries
between information or entertainment and propaganda.

In fact, commercial messages create a new way of storytelling that
blends people and events, language and ideas with multiple purposes
and endings into a new genre. Its purpose is to serve what Edward
Bernays called in 1947 the "engineering of consent," a new process
of achieving democracy through purposeful and scientific methods.
He described the freedom to persuade as the very essence of a
democratic process that is guaranteed by the constitution.

His advertising manifesto provided unparalleled power over the
means of communication and – in its service to politics – an agenda
for promoting a new market. The rise of political advertising
suggested the packaging and sale of political ideas, not unlike other
consumer goods. It reduced the participatory aspects of political
debate to a sales event, in which culture served to reinforce authority, while mass communication provided the language of domination. In addition, political advertising constituted a welcome source
of revenue for media industries, which strengthened the ties
between economic and political interests, often at the expense of
journalistic autonomy and the representation of alternative social or
political views; the result was an infringement on freedom of choice.

A still broader approach to advertising must consider the steady breakdown of lines of demarcation between genres, not unlike those between journalism and literature, when persuasion materializes in a variety of mass communication messages, from film and broadcasting imagery to the printed words of fact and fiction. The result is a culturally consistent and total presence of (ideological) perspectives that reinforce particular visions of the world.

Thus, the process of mass communication becomes subject to commercial and political claims on the nature and extent of social practices that privilege those with access to the media industries, whose own assertions of objectivity or fairness, truth, and freedom drive the contemporary engineering of public consent. The latter is based on the production and dissemination of social knowledge and its control.

IV

Indeed, mass communication constitutes an appropriate and effective process of reproducing knowledge and experience that is aided by the popularity of the written word. With it comes the lure of inclusiveness for those skilled in the art of reading – one of the essential human practices of sharing social knowledge. In fact, for St Augustine the eye constitutes the world's point of entry; in this he was following Cicero, who noted that texts are better seen than heard in order to be remembered. Hence, gathering, interpreting, and disseminating information quickly develops from being a primary activity of literate individuals to a collective exercise, when new means of mass communication, such as visual imagery, offer revolutionary ways of reaching into society and beyond to span the world.

People live in social formations that determine the system of social knowledge in which they participate and through which, ultimately, they seek to liberate themselves. Indeed, social knowledge, according to Socrates, sets the individual free and has meaning only if it contributes to improving the daily lives of people. Providing opportunities for participation in the acquisition and use of social knowledge is the function of mass communication in its educational role. Furthermore, the desire for social knowledge leads to a search for truth and to a scientific perspective on the world. The eternal search for truth becomes a scientific challenge, or as Herbert Marcuse concludes – after analyzing Max Weber's work – truth becomes criticism, which turns into accusation and becomes the focus of scientific inquiry.

Mass communication, from its beginnings, has been associated with the production and dissemination of social knowledge, that is, with a form of pragmatic knowledge that pertains to what people accept as real. Consequently, the social world attains its meaning through different interpretations of common experiences, arising from ideological perspectives, such as political, cultural, generational, or class differences. According to Karl Marx (and other classical sociologists) social knowledge is significantly influenced by the predominant forms of social organization, whose prevailing ideas are grounded in a collaboration of social scientific, political, and educational forces and rely on the process of mass communication to help reinforce the ideological thrust of a particular world view. These observations corroborate current engagements of mass communication and the production of what we know about the world. Mass communication helps introduce, popularize, and reinforce specific versions of a social reality that is consensual by design as it sets the social or cultural agenda under the influence of a given economic and political order.

But since human knowledge, as Ernst Cassirer reminds us, is comprised of symbolic knowledge, the arising notions of meaning and meaning-making direct our attention to the territory of culture, where individual agency reproduces a social world that reflects, not a static or objective reality, but rather a particular ideologically determined actuality. More specifically, a critical conceptualization of social knowledge, according to Jürgen Habermas, must differentiate between "technical" and "practical" knowledge. Thus, the purposive-rational action of capitalism stresses the technical and marginalizes the capacity for communicative action which involves issues of human conduct. The manifestation of technical knowledge in the institutional framework of mass communication refers either to decisions regarding rules of conduct or to instrumental action to help organize the appropriate means of controlling the idea of mass communication.

The desire for practical knowledge, on the other hand, relates to the intersubjectivity of mutual understandings regarding the role and function of mass communication in social intercourse. It is secured by the mutual obligations of a trusting relationship that is directed towards enlightenment and, ultimately, towards emancipation. Practical knowledge also refers to understanding the cultural and historical conditions of mass communication, the economic consequences of commercial practices, the material circumstances of mass communication as a social process, and their impact on the ideological framework of society. It is a knowledge that thrives on contributions of individual thought, or on intellectual freedom generally, beyond the indoctrinating power of mass communication in an environment free from domination by a universe of societal expectations that reinforce and perpetuate the dominant ideology.

Still, mass communication is determined by the ruling ideas of political and economic forces, and is, therefore, focused on the production of consent and compliance rather than on the autonomy of the individual. Since its production of social knowledge advances the cause of a dominant order, mass communication is the carrier of technical knowledge to help organize and control society through standardization and mass production in a lasting process of assimilation that is of considerable historical significance in its duration and resolution.

In other words, recognizing the importance of media and the process of mass communication in the social and political development of society is as old as the earliest media – for instance, from newsletters produced by the House of Fugger in Germany (itself an expression of the capitalism of the age) or newsbooks in Britain, to the spread of literature across Europe. The latter reproduced ideas, provided a forum for private thought, and familiarized feudal societies with the world. Yet printing also reinforced a split between a literate, cultured class and the illiterate masses still chained to the world of sound – including the voices of storytellers and their contributions to a growing popular literature – until the eighteenth century, when educational reforms swept through the Western world.

Accompanied by an uprooting of tastes and a revolt against the prerogatives of a cultured class, mass communication finally conquered new social strata in European society, and new markets, when the "barbarians" could read and enter the realm of the privileged. The presence of a shared language – and the ability to read and understand, with an increased use of the vernacular – not only supplied a basis for establishing relations among people or transmitting information in the interest of mass enlightenment, but also provided opportunities for manipulation and the enforcement of social control.

Thus, mass communication in its historical role advanced the hope for inclusion – and certainly of participation – in the ideational life of society. It also raised expectations of political liberation from the authority of those in control of the printed word. In fact, the printed word had been the foundation of an authoritarian rule of church and state as it delivered power over ignorance and became the key to the contentment of social, cultural, and political elites in their role of knowledge brokers. Literacy effectively splits and controls societies, when priests and bureaucrats share in the articulation of reality through word and print and compellingly define and trade social knowledge.

But mass communication, however welcome as a means of spreading the authoritarian ideologies of church and state, also expanded the cause of literacy. On its course towards a vernacular and cosmopolitan future, literacy destroyed the institutional hold on knowledge and changed its relation to class. Accordingly, mass communication offered mobility across class lines in the process of sharing knowledge, and reinforced the natural curiosity of people by providing insights into the social and political thoughts and practices of various elites.

There is a price to pay, however, for access to ideas when the printed word turned into a new commodity. Consequently, texts were efficiently manufactured and sold for a wide variety of purposes – ranging from information or knowledge to organized distraction or political manipulation – while they were protected like property in their fictional or nonfictional combinations. The new author, recently separated from the comforts of patronage or institutional affiliation, engaged in a new economic form of intellectual work – although a free market for intellectual goods did not appear until the eighteenth century (in England) or even later elsewhere.

In the meantime, words (and images) were packaged to promote specific ideological positions, while knowledge and interest in the social and political practices of a democratic society – together with a need for distraction in an increasingly industrialized environment – were the principal forces behind the rise of mass communication markets.

The accessibility of a range of ideas not only reinforced the natural curiosity of individuals and promoted a societal discourse, but also strengthened the myth of social and cultural empowerment, which was perpetuated by the idea of a free press, in particular, as a spontaneous response to censorship and control of the flow of knowledge, or to the proprietary uses of public information. The latter frequently made political interests unaccountable to the public and contributed to the decreasing credibility of mass communication. Thus, banning books was the most direct and public form of censorship; it suggested authoritatively what people should not read, but, even more importantly, what they should not think. Modern forms of mass communication, in the guise of press or broadcasting practices, contain a far more hidden form of censorship with roots in the ideological preferences of owners and in a professional culture of compliance among journalists and creative workers, which produces self-censorship.

Nevertheless, universal access to knowledge is a prerequisite for conceptualizing an active public whose opinions become the basis for participation in the social or political life of society. Hence, the idea of public opinion emerged from the potential of mass communication in the process of democratization.

V

Cultural conservatives may have regretted the newly acquired access of the masses to the printed word (and therefore to knowledge), immediately followed by the arrival of new types of entertainment and information that catered not only to curiosity, but also to a fascination with living in a much larger and more complicated world than people could have imagined without the help of literature or journalism. Others called it progress and a confirmation of democratic principles; they pointed to the role of a free press, the rise of public opinion, and individual freedom to choose in a marketplace of ideas.

Indeed, mass communication as a technology of dissemination accommodated expanding demands for knowledge in an increasingly complex world, which, in turn, created a need for more markets and encouraged specialization. At the start of the nineteenth century, media had become sufficiently equipped to help advance the cause of journalism as a popularizer of ideas and entertainer of the masses with a creative mix of fact and fiction that found its way into information and opinion. Habermas speaks of the bourgeois public sphere, which emerged earlier from a new social order, based on the need for information regarding commerce – and capitalism in general – and the rise of the social as an expression of mutual dependence in the public realm. With this also came an increase in confidence in the judgment of common people, or faith in rationalism, which is an acknowledgment of the idea of public opinion as an expression of an enlightened mass. The term was actually coined in the late eighteenth century with the growth of populations in urban centers, the increase in literacy, and the development of mass communication, that is, the duplication and circulation of large numbers of pamphlets or posters. However, the opinion process actually emerged in the fifteenth century, after the introduction of printing and with the Reformation, which not only questioned clerical authority, but signaled a widespread concern over religious issues, political changes, and the spread of ideologies of progress.

Indeed, the notion of public opinion signaled the arrival of a new authority. Celebrated by some (Bryce) and denounced by others (Marx), the idea of public opinion became a manifestation of an individual's social or political presence in the public realm. Ferdinand Tönnies spoke about public opinion as the expression of a public will and considered the press a manufacturer of opinions and an indispensable "printed marketplace." He joined others, such as Gabriel Tarde and Gustave Le Bon, who also addressed the idea of public opinion in the context of European urbanization and industrialization to reserve its place in the conceptualization of a democratic society.

There is also a need to account for the presence of the masses amidst political claims of emancipation, when the expression of opinions becomes a sign of participation. Regardless of the size and social structure of the public – which changed significantly from the Middle Ages to modern times – expressions of the public mind have continued to interest social theorists as evidence of social or political activities, particularly in light of the role of mass communication in constructing social and political realities.

Aided by technological advances and through the spread of literacy and the questioning of clerical authority during the Reformation, public opinion prospered with the rise of reason as a new authority. The latter elevated the role of individuals as a source of ideas and opinions and promoted the ascent of the modern idea of the public. Indeed, it is at this point in the cultural history of mass communication that the idea of communication, in general, becomes identified with the task of uniting and sustaining societies. Since the utilization of the printing press in the discourse of society, systems of communication had typically accompanied the evolution of the public sphere, public opinion, and democracy, and would play a major role in the (political) use of mass communication during the twentieth century. Furthermore, the production of public opinion – thought to arise from individuals or relevant groups or organizations in society – shifted into the realm of the media, which manufactured public opinion vis-à-vis social or political institutions in a process that eliminated the original sources. Walter Lippmann, for instance, reminded his readers in the 1920s that public opinion, in order to be sound, should be organized for the press and not by the press, as was the case already at that time.

Nevertheless, mass communication emerged as a major force in the production, circulation, and interpretation of public opinion; it facilitated the creation of political or ideological positions, absorbed individual opinions into the process of societal communication, and fashioned language to reach large constituencies that participated – at least potentially – in the public opinion process, creating the illusion that they had been heard or taken into account. In other words, mass communication helped build consensus through adaptation and integration of differing interests.

Moreover, public opinion became a valuable intellectual product with the rise of polling and an interest in prediction and control of opinions – especially for political purposes, like elections. Polling turned into a lucrative business, the credibility of whose social scientific methods only added to its success with politics and commerce, both always eager to know the outcome of their respective campaigns. Yet there are problems with its principal claim to be able to measure opinions about complex subjects when communicative competence, expert understanding, and historical consciousness are missing from the intellectual make-up of a contemporary society (or where they are incomplete). Thus, the response of audiences whose education lacks depth, whose interests are vague, and whose knowledge is technical rather than practical, may jeopardize the intent of a question. Immersed in the world of mass communication, which is the world of commodified distractions, individuals most likely react with knowledge about the immediate, which rewards spontaneity, but lacks thoughtfulness.

Public opinion polling is a form of mass communication that benefited from the rising popularity of science in the nineteenth century and from the subsequent reduction of all fields of knowledge to the dimensions of a natural science. It is cultivated by pollsters (and journalists) and recreated with scientific methods that are compatible with earlier definitions of the individual as a machine and the world as a mechanism. These ideas reappear in organismic theories of society – such as Comte's idea of society as a collective organism with structure and specialized functions – which treat communication as a binding force in society and public opinion as a response that reflects the real needs of the masses. Since public opinion deals with matters developed in the minds of others, it is incapable of producing new ideas, or even recognizing them, before they are presented. Mass communication, whether or not it creates or manipulates public opinion, converts pending questions of relevance or meaning into statements of fact through the act of publication, when public opinion becomes real, and reality demands a response.

The pursuit of public opinion is the concrete manifestation of a fundamental shift of the culture of mass communication (in the

United States) from historical explanation to scientific analysis. This trend – which has made inroads into European and Asian cultures – is reflected in a primary interest in opinions and opinion-making rather than in knowledge or systems of knowledge, with an insistence on the significance of aggregates of information or empirically verifiable relations of ideas that rely on a lack of historical context to focus on the immediacy of the moment.

Mass communication meets the requirements of a scientific outlook that embraces the consequences of the scientific process rather than engaging in a search for its historical sources. Thus, speculative or impressionistic thought regarding the historical position of mass communication has been replaced by questions about its impact or effect. Journalism became an important arena for testing the effectiveness of an ensuing ideological discourse that would change traditional relations between media and society.

VI

Thus, with the nineteenth century drawing to a close, the means of mass communication became identified with specific demands of consumption: books and academic journals for a cultural elite, newspapers and magazines for a general public, the stage for literary crowds, and movies for illiterates or immigrants, and a new industrial middle class, whose hunger for entertainment spawned a popular culture industry that would ignite an ideological struggle between supporters of high and low culture in the 1950s. In fact, mass communication identifies and defines class interests by catering to particular taste cultures in society, which reinforces class differences and which led, two generations later, to a distinct separation of interests and knowledge regarding media uses and the process of mass communication.

Although local culture still benefited from these developments at the beginning of the twentieth century, which promised social and technological progress – local newspapers prevailed, as did local theaters or movie houses and local clubs with local musical talent abounding – there were signs of consolidation, with an expanding national culture on the horizon.

The industrialization of mass communication began with the demise of an artisan culture – the printer as intellectual worker – and ended with the centralized production of books and movies, for example on America's East Coast and in Hollywood and New York, respectively. For instance, the widespread use of merchandizing catalogs in the acculturation of new and old immigrants – a sign of access to distant communities – signaled the imminent death of an autonomous local culture, while the rotary press, telephone, and typewriter created new forms of domination. Those who owned and applied these means of communication subjugated others, including journalists and printers, to industrial technologies of production and dissemination. The subsequent dependencies, accompanied by a division of labor, relegated journalists to wage laborers and shifted claims of press freedom from intellectual workers to ownership. George Gerbner's phrase that the media are "the cultural arms of the industrial order from which they spring" is an apt description of these developments. In a society where the means of mass communication are manufacturing plants of cultural goods, the idea of work becomes central to an understanding of the modern artist or journalist as worker hovering over the conveyor belt of a culture industry. Creative, intellectual work turns into mass production, while individual ideas undergo ideological scrutiny to fit the demands of the market, where predictability and repetition are the key to commercial success.

Now too large, too populated, and too culturally diverse, the United States returned to earlier interests in social control, sought to promote political harmony, and pushed for economic expansion, which – besides real or imagined dangers from abroad – turned into the major concerns of the twentieth century. Culture became the field of operation, and mass communication provided the means of adaptation and incorporation. One is reminded here of Gramsci's writings about the cultural sphere during the 1920s, which coincide with European debates about realism and modernism and suggest that culture is the result of a complex process of elaboration, which includes the potential role of elites in the manipulation of popular consciousness to reach consensus through media, education, or culture in general. Mass communication practices – with their technical facility to overcome geographical distances and their use of psychological expertise to establish ideological consent – played a decisive role in the processing of culture for the benefit of a stable and predictable political system.

For instance, the development of radio broadcasting in the United States, with its centralizing function of networks (later extended to television), contributed immeasurably to the development of a national taste culture, not only with the production and marketing of entertainment genres, but also with the dissemination of news and information. These efforts were reinforced with the later invention of mobile technologies – such as the automobile radio or transistor radios and portable television sets – which increased the accessibility (and captivity) of audiences across the nation.

Questions of what is news or what it is important for society to know came to be decided by broadcasting organizations, mass-circulation newspapers, and magazines and their respective operators. They are reinforced by an emerging visual culture, beginning in the 1920s and defined by picture magazines and Hollywood movies. Technological progress, such as rotary presses, telephones, or FM radio and television, or the introduction of color in the process of mass communication, translated efficiently and effectively into commercially viable means of communication, which served to enlarge and reinforce a modern consumer culture in support of mass markets. Invaluable for the creation of consumer demand, mass communication increased the traffic in entertainment and information without major changes in style or content between these genres.

The concomitant centralization of production and dissemination – less variety and fewer sources and channels of distribution – raised questions about the function of mass communication in (political) attempts to implement social control through uniformity of content and presentation across all major forms of media. These questions have become particularly acute since the number of owners of media outlets has been decreasing in the United States, while the proliferation of broadcast channels and newspapers or magazines is still quite remarkable. Thus, it has become easier to exert influence on a steadily decreasing number of proprietors or their agents. In addition, diversification has created an ownership by outside business interests, whose political ambitions may well lie elsewhere, perhaps even outside the concerns of the traditional fourth estate. Mass communication has changed under these external conditions, especially in its journalistic guise, as business interests – by sustaining higher profits – have created new demands on the craft of journalism. These have been expressed through recent efforts to market the notion of public journalism.

For instance, corporate efforts have resulted in a crusade for responsive journalism regarding the change of local news coverage, with serious consequences, not only for the profession, but also for society and the relationship of information, knowledge, and democracy. They not only suggest a new system of gathering and distributing information but imply – more fundamentally – a new authority for defining the nature and type of information that provides the basis of social and political decision-making. The result is a new partisanship that responds primarily to the needs of commerce and industry rather than to the social, economic, or political requirements of an informed public. For instance, there is serious concern among journalists, according to Thomas Leonard, based on the observation that editors and reporters are often instructed that readers are consumers or subjects rather than citizens.

Public journalism – despite its claims – is not an emancipatory movement, but exposes – through its proponents – a range of limitations that deny the possibility of radical change in the public interest. It neither offers readers access to authorship in order to confirm their expert standing in the community, nor encourages the pursuit of public interest journalism under new forms of ownership. Public journalism does not revitalize investigative journalism or insist on a new understanding of professionalism that frees journalists from editorial controls and acknowledges their professional independence. And under no circumstances is journalism constructed as intellectual labor. To make a difference, public journalism must be freed from principles of profitability to serve the need for human communication rather than the desire for economic gain.

Yet in fact the media are still fashioned and controlled by capital. C. Wright Mills once concluded that writers as hired practitioners of an information industry are directed by decisions of others and not by their own integrity, because technical, economic, and social structures – owned and operated by others – stand between the intellectual and a potential public. Mills reminds us that freedom is without public value if it is not exercised, and that the exercise must remain in the hands of responsible journalists to claim press freedom for themselves and not for industrial interests.

Thus, current accounts of public journalism are reminiscent of progressive ideas about the need to improve the conditions for democracy without questioning the part capitalism has played in the demise of the social system. Unfortunately, these conditions seem to have worsened and it turns out that the problems of journalism reflect the problems of society. Thus, disillusionment among journalists and their reported cynicism are symptoms of widespread alienation and disbelief, while dissatisfaction with work (and pay) in the face of shifting requirements concerning the type and quality of intellectual labor in the media industries are indications of fundamental social and economic changes in society and their effects on the workplace.

VII

Throughout these developments, however, the growth of media networks and the consolidation of mass communication into fewer and larger organizations has been accompanied by reflections about the promises of a communal past and the workings of democratic practices. There is a strategy to support present policies or ideological positions with specific references to a past in which community constituted a durable manifestation of sociality with commonsensical behavior. Therefore, nostalgia enables a convergence that features the idea of community and provides the context for rationalizing, if not enforcing, ways of defining mass communication as a mutual or shared experience of service – but this time for commerce and politics.

Indeed, American folklore and literature are rich in tales about "place," pastoral villages, or small towns – all synonyms for community – which go beyond the purely geographical or physical to address a way of life, a spirit of commitment, collective identity, or a commonality of interests. Although they are not identical, politics, like communication, remain inseparable from community and are part of the cultural context, in which individuals participate, involved with each other in the public affairs of their respective localities. Such participation has been reinforced and promoted by local media, typically the local newspaper (or, later, local radio), which specializes in hometown events and in local people, with little regard for the outside world. The weekly newspaper, a surviving American institution – although now changing under markedly different economic conditions – has become the public forum for its editor, as chronicler and speaker for the community, and its readers, as participants in the weekly narratives about their world. The fact that the local press has turned into a confessional form with communal participation, according to McLuhan, adds to its popularity as a source of human interest material.

Mass communication in early America – in its technical sense of reaching large numbers of people – occurred under these circumstances as a form of communal conversation. When editors and journalists of the weekly press are joined by their readers, they interpret a world they all understand, because their encounters are for the most part immediate and collective. Readers have firsthand knowledge of facts or truths, and their familiarity with the territory of the journalistic narrative gives them expert standing not only in the community, but also in the eyes of country editors. Likewise, novelists, as chroniclers of people and events and participants in the life of the community, reveal the secrets they know, raise moral questions, and predict the future within the boundaries of the culture. All of them, readers and writers, are, in fact, expert participants in the process of mass communication.

Through times of urbanization, alienation, and loss of identity, the notion of community has maintained its symbolic power, as an anxiety-ridden society recalled the value of tradition and authority in its quest for moral certainty. The idealization of communal life – focused on harmony, including harmony with nature, and informed by a belief in order and perfection – included communication as the process of achieving understanding and agreement regarding issues of coexistence, mutual support, and survival vis-à-vis external forces. In fact, John Winthrop, aboard the *Arbell* bound for New England in 1630, identified these features of a communal existence when he urged his fellow travelers that to delight in each other and to make each other's conditions their own meant to be cognizant of being part of a community.

His remarks reflect the centrality of the social group and its characteristics and reiterate the importance of such notions as allegiance, solidarity, and tradition, which have occupied the literature of many ages, although he may not have anticipated that these values would be reflected in the political rhetoric of the republic for the next three centuries, or engage the imagination of writers, artists, and social philosophers for many generations. Among them is Charles Peirce, for whom the community becomes the vehicle of truth, incompatible with the affirmation of the private self, and a suitable environment for sharing ideas. Communication and making meaning gain their significance in the context of addressing one's thoughts to the future thoughts of other individuals. Peirce suggested that, to avoid negation, an individual as a conscious, intelligent being must address the thoughts of a community of other thinkers. His argument implies an almost religious commitment to the community, but it also suggests a connection to more contemporary conditions of culture.

Similarly for Josiah Royce, democracy was a question of organizing a community which makes this possible, while George Herbert Mead's understanding of democracy rested on the values of community. And then there is John Dewey, who insisted that the idea of democracy was the idea of community life itself. These proponents and others, for whom the connection of communication and community was the foundation of their social philosophies, also emerged as critics of their social and economic environment. They spoke up in the midst of celebrations of the spirit of individualism in the growth of industrial capitalism.

With the expansion of the United States, in particular, and the founding of hundreds of villages and small towns across the continent, began a struggle between those traditional values of community and the challenges to the ideal of a separate or distinct existence amidst social and economic change in rural America. A tidal wave of urbanization and industrialization hit rural America between 1865 and 1917, with better road systems, the automobile, mail-order houses, rural free delivery, telegraph, and telephone, but also with metropolitan newspapers, magazines, and books. The privilege of the local newspaper as the ultimate source of information or entertainment ceased with access to urban newspapers, movies, dime novels, and a general increase in mobility. Consequently, the local press adjusted in form and content to new demands with a coverage that reflected disintegration or regret over a lost sense of community.

At the same time, there was an awakening to the pettiness and triviality associated with the experience of place. It is well reflected in Edgar Lee Masters's 1915 *Spoon River Anthology*, in which the author attacks the hypocrisies of a small community. Later Sinclair Lewis and Sherwood Anderson continued to remind their readers of the deceptions and pressures of small-town life, while Thornstein Veblen mused over the transition from land as place to land as property, or competition with neighboring cities, and the dire consequences for Main Street. Still later, American sociologists, such as Robert Park or Robert and Helen Lynd, among others, who shared an interest in the historically significant conditions of community life in the United States, examined its various structures – in the form of bohemias, slums, rural settings, or suburbia, for instance – and their emergence from urbanization. They also observed the nature of the press. For Park, the newspaper was not a wholly rational product, and understanding it meant to see it in its historic perspective. The Lynds described the operations of the community press, walled in by a "free press" tradition with high obligations to report all the news, the community's expectation of a fearless press, and financial controls with dependence on advertising and the predictable performance of editors as hired hands.

Despite the critique of community in the wake of its collapse due to the inevitability of modernization, however, the quest for community and its values remains alive, and reappears in the city, ready to inspire commerce, industry and political discourse. It is a longing for the communal state, the environment of the political party or association, and the promise of companionship and security that survive radical change and become a recurring theme in representations of contemporary life. The notion of community is incorporated in such phrases as "business community," which offer a substitute environment for the original locality, which has become a desolate place. Others, like Dewey, would express a longing for the "Great Community" and recall the close relationship between communication and community as the center of a democratic existence.

However, there are other differences. Mass communication lacks the dialogical nature of communal conversations, the luxury of time, and the convenience of short distances to bring the message forward into the community. Indeed, it deprives the individual of these functions. Instead, mass communication facilitates the translation of such aspirations by reproducing a sense of participation and communal belonging with almost religious intensity.

In fact, contemporary media are also postmodern places of worship as they drift through time and space, containing fragments of people and events, without memory or historical consciousness. The popular arts replace religion in the process of mass communication and confirm Max Weber's insights into the rise of modern society, when art supersedes religion. Mass communication facilitates the ascension of the new gods of mass culture, who rise in quick succession to preach their sermons, while devoted audiences flock around them to affirm their status as disciples, or fans, reminiscent of their behavior as congregations in the lap of their communities.

Dewey once suggested that art is the most effective mode of communication; mass communication has proven the effectiveness of the popular arts in the discourse of society. It features television as a reinforcer of a consumerist ideology that has held the United States in its grip since the 1950s with situation comedies, game shows, and soap operas. Commercials still reinforce the vision of a good life, promote consumer choice as a synonym for freedom, and rely on the credibility of what Leo Lowenthal calls the idols of consumption, e.g., pop stars and celebrities. Indeed, there seems to be more trust in the words or deeds of mass-produced celebrities of film or television – and certainly more admiration for them – than in political or religious authorities, unless the latter reinvent their assigned roles in society and become celebrities as well.

In fact, the visual coverage of the subject or event, coupled (in news reporting) with the personality of the presenter, constitute the pillars of television's credibility as a trustworthy source and shape the definition of truth that dominates the societal discourse. Excluded from knowing, audiences rely on the accuracy or factuality of mass communication by what they see (read, or hear) and by the identity (and credibility) of sources. It is a referential value that is based on matching information with events, both represented, however, through mass communication. Thus, truth has become a matter of trust in pronouncements about the state of affairs that are produced by the media; they originate with popular emissaries of the industry, whose own expert sources are typically selected from within a narrow ideological range of experts. Mass communication therefore not only creates the social or political realities in which people live, but confirms these realities by supplying reliability (or consistency) and the comforts of knowing the truth.

The products of mass communication are a contiguous text that combines commercial and political propaganda, information, and entertainment to offer instant gratification in a communal atmosphere that appeals to individuals, who are caught in a historically determined drift of social relationships. The media are friend and companion, and fulfill, according to Henk Prakke (speaking of television), an *amicus* function, which focuses on the intimate relationship between audiences and their favorite programs or celebrities. Radio personalities and movie stars earlier in the twentieth century had offered similar comforts to an alienated public – not to speak of pinup girls and male crooners, or characters in famous novels. In either case, mass communication functions as the cultural or social setting in which individuals, grounded in the community of fans, express and reinforce their feelings of belonging.

In the meantime, the local as a social reality, or as a source of theoretical claims of authentic communication, has receded into the pages of early twentieth-century history. Instead, mobility, heterogeneity, and centralization have demolished commonalities among people and led to the rise of mass society. Along the way, theorists such as Frédéric Le Play and Emile Durkheim noticed a disintegration and atomization of society – reflecting Karl Marx's observations of the role of the bourgeoisie in the change from familial to money relations – and industrialization disturbed the pastoral settings of social theory. Later Ferdinand Tönnies described the change from *Gemeinschaft* to *Gesellschaft* as an inevitable move from a social order that is founded on harmony to one that rests on convention and agreement and is ideologically justified in public opinion. Similarly, Durkheim spoke of mechanic and organic solidarity, Robert

Redfield developed a folk–urban dichotomy, and Howard Becker constructed sacred and secular societies to suggest the changing features of Western societies. The modern version is an urban life that features commercial instead of communal relations and a separation along lines of mass communication.

Mass communication grew with these developments; it became an urban phenomenon – with a debilitated and marginalized rural tradition in its wake. It continues to change under rapidly developing technological and industrial influences to serve an urban population, while achieving symbolic significance as a representation of communal aspirations by reproducing a sense of familiarity.

Mobility – another synonym for the process of mass communication – produced change and shaped modernization. Fueled by migration and expanding in many directions, societal movement materialized upwards in skyscrapers and airplanes and horizontally in roads and urban sprawl, while absorbing and redirecting the notion of community. Along this path, commercial interests employed mass communication to successfully respond to the communal longings of a mobile society by simulating common features that implied the realization of a democratic life.

In other words, the media seized upon the enduring need for a sense of community and acknowledged the desire for belonging by operationalizing the idea of sharing or partaking in creative ways that would also enhance the idea of democratic practice, but which actually promoted consumption as a routinized form of participation in the (commercial) life of society. The success of participation relies on cultural standardization – resulting in the widespread sharing of values, beliefs, and tastes among diverse social groups; it is aided by mass literacy and popular education and most effectively operationalized and sustained by mass communication.

Beyond the impact of mass communication on traditional ideas of community, including the community of journalists, however, there is the rise of social criticism, which accompanies mass communication on the path of industrialization and media capitalism.

VIII

The birth of mass communication as an American ideology of technological progress in the service of democracy occurred in an atmosphere of industrial practices – vis-à-vis the demands of commercial and military conflicts. It was accompanied by the rise of a new social scientific curiosity about social control. Indeed, Gramsci's suggestion that social (or political) control is a matter of incorporation is reflected in earlier considerations of the power of public opinion, or the role of the press, for instance, when censorship as a common political practice was replaced by the use of persuasion and co-optation that depended on the use of mass communication.

Thus, since the end of the nineteenth century there has been a shift among newspapers from being a political institution – with a peculiar, often personal, agenda, party loyalty, and individual editorial leadership that signal partisanship and awareness of an anticipating, loyal readership – to a market orientation with the goal of catering to a large and anonymous readership with diverse political interests. In this change of character, mass communication took advantage of the commodification or standardization of news and – more generally – reflected the structural changes of industrialization that would eventually lead to the consolidation and concentration of ownership – not just of the press, but also of broadcasting and film. As means of mass communication continued to be combined in the hands of fewer owners – and few attempts have been made recently to address the issues of one-newspaper towns, chain ownership, or broadcast networks and cross-ownership – one discovers with Barzan and Sweeney (in *Monopoly Capital*) that monopoly rather than competition determines capitalism. Indeed, mass communication thrives under conditions of industrialization.

Michael Schudson calls these developments the "antithesis of association or community." They narrow the potential of the public sphere and strengthen the commitment to profitability and economic survival. Consequently, a neglect of the community at large at the expense of class differences, ethnic diversity, social conflict resolution, and the potential for widespread participation in the public discourse, creates a media system that is more committed to private profitability than to public accountability.

45

These developments have been accompanied by a need for social (or political) control, which produces ideas about what to do to people rather than about what people could do for themselves with the means of communication to meet the promise of personal advancement and social well-being. The result is a new vision of a democratic future that insists on reinforcing the notion that the media serve power – allegedly for the public good – rather than aid empowerment. The manifestation of this vision in the corporatization of society strengthens the centralization of reality construction as a collective effort, for instance, by news agencies and leading media organizations.

The ideological perspective in mass communication appears with its political practice of defending individual freedom (and the principles of a free press) and of confirming a belief in serving democracy. The latter, combined with the prestige of technology, reinforces the myth of a strong and independent media system. However, as a cultural practice, mass communication remains subject to the social, political, and economic forces by which society is shaped and defined, confirming its supportive role and function in the arsenal of the dominant power structure and, therefore, its dependence on the overarching institutional relations of politics and commerce.

These conditions have not gone unnoticed in the United States, but the consistent, and sometimes blatant, criticism – from Upton Sinclair to Noam Chomsky – of mass communication during the twentieth century, has rarely touched the public in any significant way. Individual protests or outright rejection are easily absorbed, and the media rely on monopolistic or oligarchic practices in their respective surroundings; they neutralize opposition and eventually force a discontented audience to return to consulting the same media for vital information about their immediate environment.

There are few, if any, alternatives. Some competing newspapers have survived in larger cities, while national broadcasting networks and cable television, in particular, carry homogenized information and entertainment. Standards of journalism, or definitions of news, are subjected to business interests, while aesthetic or creative considerations in entertainment yield to market demands. Even exceptions – such as the Public Broadcasting System, a few publishers of books or small magazines, and independent radio stations as potential platforms for a public critique of mass communication – must depend on government funding and private donations and are still subject to commercially determined agendas.

Quite recently journalists have joined the chorus of mostly academic voices, which condemn the lack of serious news, or of in-depth coverage of domestic and foreign affairs. Yet, even the latest critique, which acknowledges the close ties between the quality of journalism and the quality of life, and calls for an accountability by the powerful, returns to visions of community and self-determination of individuals for solutions to problems that are systemic and the outcome of commercial interests in a capitalist society.

For instance, Leonard Downie Jr. and Robert G. Kaiser suggest, in *The News about the News,* that the fate of news will ultimately be determined by what people decide to do about their country, implying competence and power on the side of a reading public whose real position, however, is socially and politically diminished. The authors also disregard the personification of corporate interests – accomplished by personal and compassionate appeals to individuals for participation in the process of mass communication. In fact, the business of mass communication is more interested in understanding how people want to be entertained than in what people need to know to make conscious and informed decisions regarding their lives in a democratic society.

Worse still is the treatment of journalists, as Howard Kurtz suggests, when prose is squeezed and controversial ideas are pasteurized and homogenized. Indeed, under current circumstances journalism is no longer a craft, but a bureaucratic assignment to produce viable, non-controversial reading or viewing materials for public consumption. Journalists as intellectual workers operate under what Max Weber calls bureaucratic management – which prevails in advanced capitalist institutions like the media – and which translates into adherence to an ordered system of subordination and control that aims for permanence. Working within a highly structured system of production, journalists become, under specific political conditions, the most important representatives of the "demagogic species," according to Weber.

It is the outrage of the day rather than the events of the day, compliance rather than controversy, kidnapping or murder as individualized tragedies rather than war, atrocities, or the environment as enduring global issues that fill newspapers and news hours in an endless and disconnected cycle of spectacles; the latter reflect the impatience of modern times, curiosity for the sake of new thrills, and relief at the lack of knowledge or interest among audiences.

In the meantime, Robert McChesney characterizes contemporary media in terms of corporate concentration, conglomeration, and hyper-commercialism, while Ben Bagdikian reports on the accelerated centralization of media power in the face of favorable economic conditions and an expanding market. Economic changes are accompanied by a shifting climate of media ownership which seems to thrive on breaking with traditional notions of public trust or public interest. Many years earlier, William Allen White observed that media owners – who pursue media ownership in search of power and prestige – seem to display an "unconscious arrogance of conscious wealth" after they make their fortunes in some other calling than journalism. In fact, the media have become part of the corporate domain of the American society which converts economic domination into political power. Thus, the media shape consciousness and help reinforce the dominant corporate ideology, which becomes the reigning political ideology.

Changes in the size and quality of media ownership have been accompanied by a considerable and long-lasting concern among intellectuals about their own predicament – which is their inability to act on what they know and foresee. What they have foreseen, however, exists as a critical observation about culture and cultural institutions in American society and provides a historical perspective on the role of the media; the observation reaches from the cultural crisis described by Lewis Corey in the 1930s to the workings of the "cultural apparatus" outlined by C. Wright Mills in the 1940s, or the "cultural mass" addressed by Daniel Bell in the 1970s – not to mention the more recent impact of British writers such as E. P. Thompson, Raymond Williams, or Stuart Hall on revitalizing critical cultural studies in the United States. Their notions of class, power, ideology, and the nature of representation, in particular, push progressive thought beyond the traditional boundaries of American pragmatism and provide opportunities for a cultural discourse, for instance, that addresses the historical realities of newsroom labor and the contemporary conditions of work as well as the public interest, among other issues.

The consolidation of media and politics has all but eliminated the notion of journalism as the fourth estate and introduces significant definitional changes to the traditional idea of journalism as a cultural practice. Indeed, the predominance of a marketing orientation in newswork results in a shifting conception of newsroom labor.

More specifically, the media have rarely been facilitators of intellectual labor free from a business-oriented paternalism that directs journalists – or writers – in their work. But the significant rise of corporate power and control over the contemporary role and function of journalists, in particular, threatens the demise of traditional notions of journalistic practices; by prescribing the manner of mass communication and redirecting the social and political purposes of the media in general, journalistic practices are being redefined to match the new expectations of the news business.

And yet, the myth of a forceful and impartial press, operating in the interest of society, prevailed throughout this period, strengthened – no doubt – by self-promotion, including the writing of celebratory histories of journalism, and by extraordinary journalistic accomplishments that have more to do with indulging the individual activities of enterprising journalists than with the social consciousness of media ownership.

Indeed, the labor of journalists has been successfully contained within the organizational media structure through a ritual of appropriation, a historical process of incorporating journalists into the system of information-gathering and news production while dominating the conditions of employment and the definition of work. Consequently, newsroom cultures are undergoing dramatic changes. Since the conditions of journalism in modernity are shaped by a shift to new technologies and new strategies of serving the information needs of specific segments of society, they make different demands on journalists and their relations to each other and to their institutions – and they affect the notion of work itself. The result is not only an increasing sense of alienation but a changing perception of what constitutes journalism and, therefore, of public interest and social responsibility at the beginning of the twenty-first century. Finally, when social and political power is constituted by information – and social knowledge – as a new form of property, class divisions occur over access to and participation in social communication.

These conditions of journalism are an outgrowth of late capitalism and the logical conclusion of a long march into a free-market system which denies collective interests and shuns collective responsibilities. Journalism is an intellectual vocation, although frequently undermined by the technical rationale of journalism education itself and the anti-intellectual orientation of many media organizations.

Intellectuals operate in a world of ideas, and their stage is the realm of the media; they occupy a specific sociopolitical role and function openly in reaction to specific areas of concern. Ralph Dahrendorf once described them as the court jesters of modern society who must doubt the obvious, suggest the relativity of authority, and ask questions that no one else dares to ask. The power of intellectuals lies in their freedom with respect to the hierarchy of the social order. They are, after all, qualified to speak on matters of culture and engage society in a critique which utters uncomfortable truths but also engages with the possibility of realizing utopian dreams.

A political challenge to curb the growing power of media industries and the corporate control of journalism, in particular, encounters the unlimited power of employers to interfere in the labor of journalists, to jeopardize their positions as intellectual workers, and, ultimately, to turn the idea of journalism into a campaign for their private vision of the world.

These visions include the larger, global claims of media industries – strengthened by the economic and political goals of commerce and government – on the role of mass communication in the service of national interests.

IX

The increasing complexity of a global existence, often treated by proponents as a communal affair, is rarely reflected in American media coverage, where news segments like the "world in a minute" or the "global minute" are the cultural indicators of foreign affairs programming. Equally inconsequential is the newspaper or news magazine coverage of genuinely global developments. This includes the tendency to report on international news primarily after a national, regional, or local angle converts stories into domestic incidents that happen to occur abroad. The net effect is a lack of information about the social, political, cultural, or economic conditions of autonomous societies elsewhere, an issue that is rarely addressed by journalists and summarily ignored by American audiences. Consequently, Americans have a selective (and superficial) knowledge of some parts of the world, which – over the years – have included Vietnam, Panama, Haiti, Kuwait, Bosnia, or more recently, Afghanistan and Iraq; these are places, where American military involvement draws media attention and results in extended conflict coverage.

Indeed, television organizations, from CNN and Fox to MSNBC, in particular, thrive on conflict, utilize sensational headlines, and employ a confirmational lingo that corroborates rather than challenges official versions of events. "We report, you decide" or "real journalism: fair and balanced" are public relations slogans intent on obscuring the ideological nature of news. Moreover, several media organizations rely on the credibility of their institution (the *New York Times* or MSNBC, respectively) or on the veracity attributed to their presentation, and perpetuate deceptions that come with slogans like "all the news that's fit to print" or "fiercely independent."

Yet there is still not much variety in content, especially within television or the press. The result is a numbing conformity of content, style, or even color schemes across the media spectrum that affects all forms of mass communication and makes the landscape of popular culture look colorful and shallow, but utterly familiar.

In this sense, there is no free press – or freedom of expression – in a society of captive audiences, where mass communication turns into an ideologically predetermined performance for the purpose of commercial gain rather than public enlightenment. Since it seems impossible to accomplish both goals, the public always receives what it wants rather then what it needs, and typically before it will know what it wants, because, the process of mass communication is also anticipatory and suggestive in its efforts to attract and retain a responsive audience.

Although this marketing strategy pertains to the essence of mass communication, journalistic practice is particularly affected by its dependence on the commercial aspirations of its medium at the expense of public service. For instance, the Commission of Freedom of the Press concluded as early as 1947 that if schools improved the standard of people's education, media responsibility to raise the level of American culture, or to supply citizens with correct political, economic, and social information, would be materially altered. Considering society a working system of ideas, the Commission insisted that people have available to them as many ideas as possible, even those not shared by the owners of the means of mass communication. Almost 60 years later the same observations hold true; what has become worse, however, is the complacency of a more powerful media industry, the increasing alienation of its workers, and the loss of a historical perspective among the public regarding the promises of a vigorous and independent press.

The current conditions of mass communication raise more fundamental questions, however, than the issue of press freedom alone, since the boundaries of press freedom may always remain contentious on legal territories such as pornography, defamation, or sedition. For example, if, as John Keane suggests, democracy is rule by publics who make their judgment in public, mass communication must not only supply expert knowledge to come to sound decisions, but it must provide the public with opportunities for sharing such judgments. It is doubtful whether most individuals are served well by the media, which rarely meet such expectations, although they may operate on the presumption of constituting a foundation of democracy. Instead, they may well be informed by selective, expert judgments, which typically appear as statements of fact rather than as contributing opinions to a public discussion. Indeed, contemporary mass communication practices demonstrate the decline of public debate in favor of expert pronouncements, which are often reduced to politically motivated soundbites that become facts. When opinion is reproduced as fact, mass communication simply serves to confirm, reinforce, or sell ideologically correct assessments or beliefs. In the long run, such practices may well breed political detachment, if not indifference, among audiences with civic ambitions but limited political power.

Mass communication in its present form matured and expanded after the end of World War II and with the beginning of the Cold War in the 1950s, when foreign markets were secured, often for political reasons, but also for an expanding economy. Aside from the export of media technologies – which created other dependencies and confirmed the commonality of a scientific language – the exportable content of mass communication ranged from information to cultural products and practices. These included eating habits (soft drinks and hamburgers), lifestyles (blue jeans and chewing gum), and music (jazz and rock 'n' roll), which were most frequently introduced with the export of Hollywood movies and, later, television series, or through the global distribution techniques of American record companies.

For instance, after the end of World War II, Americans and Russians provided scores of movies for the entertainment of a defeated Germany to promote capitalism and socialism, respectively. Both sides had quickly realized that with mass communication technologies one could reach almost anybody and create almost any illusion to respond effectively to those who needed to dream of a better life (in suburbia or on a collective farm). A generation later, the spread of American movies and television dramas ensures a constant presence of the American way of life around the world.

With it has spread a free-market ideology – throughout western Europe and much of the postcolonial world – that inaugurated (or duplicated) the model of legally protected private ownership of the means of communication and opened new markets for the distribution of cultural goods. Mass communication packages the values and visions of an American or Western lifestyle for unimpeded distribution under the mandate of a "free flow of information" to economically weak nations. Executed in the spirit of friendship or good will, it amounts to thinly disguised economic expansion. And it works.

For instance, the idea of a "free flow of information" has been a political objective – supported by UNESCO – that eases unrestricted trade, including the flow of cultural goods through channels of mass communication, for purposes of creating favorable social or political conditions of controlling the production of everyday realities. This was particularly relevant in light of the East–West conflict, when propaganda, commercial appeals, and cultural advances combined into a powerful and persuasive narrative.

The result has been a rebirth of the empire, this time determined by superior media technologies and the realization among politicians and business leaders that mass communication is the sine qua non of any successful strategy of economic expansion and political domination. It is an old idea, of course, that gains new significance with the advances in communication technologies and the political and economic status of the United States as a superpower with physical and political access to much of the world. Thus, the success of mass communication is guaranteed not only by a favorable political climate, but also by the ample supply of a cultural narrative that is rooted in advertising, journalism, and entertainment. In fact, the United States has become the major supplier of information and general broadcast programming at rates that are significantly lower than original production costs, since foreign sales typically constitute bonus revenues.

About 60 years since it began, the spread of American mass communication has turned into a permanent process of reinforcing the Americanization (or Westernization) of cultures, or of cultural leveling that characterizes a move towards "globalization." The step into a global existence is a process that was identified earlier as cultural imperialism, an ambiguous term but one with strong political appeal for those opposed to the one-directional flow of cultural goods. A cultural imperialism thesis, according to Jeremy Tunstall, condemns the disappearance of authentic, traditional and local cultures in parts of the world because of Western efforts of an indiscriminate, mass dumping of commercial and media products.

This process, far from being new in the history of the world, becomes problematic when the United States, in particular – and Western nations generally – dominate the flow of cultural goods. Its political undertones – called "Americanization" in the 1920s, cultural imperialism in the 1960s, and globalization in the twenty-first century – threaten the cultural autonomy of other nations and their decisions regarding cultural exchanges. Although cultures thrive on openness, they require cultural interaction for enhancing the idea of progress or modernization.

Differently expressed, the territorial struggles of the nineteenth and early twentieth centuries with their military occupation – or the revolutionary movements in more recent years that conquered radio or television stations long before suppressing any physical resistance – have been replaced successfully by an infiltration of cultural goods, whose effectiveness leads to a homogenization (or Westernization) of cultures – more recently like those in eastern Europe.

The Cold War victory, in other words, was won by cultural means rather than military options; or, as Thomas Pynchon describes it in *Gravity's Rainbow*, modern wars are always waged between media, communication technologies, and data streams. This new course of aggression and domination features the arena of mass communication as the ideological battleground in the fight for the hearts and minds of people. It is a struggle for consensus with the means of mass persuasion, including the attraction of cultural goods, such as music, films, or literature.

In fact, cultural imperialism in its more abstract form refers to the rise of capitalism, the development of markets, and the process of modernity, when strong historical forces – as nations – insist on defining progress and on promoting their credibility domestically as well as abroad. It also reflects the move from an industrial stage of economic development to an information (and service) stage with a central role for the means of mass communication in the domain of production, where industrial growth and expansion shift to the spread of information and knowledge as forms of control. In other words, cultural imperialism does not act only in pursuit of intended goals, as is often claimed, but is a more general consequence of expansion and a byproduct of a specific economic order, like a free-market system, that becomes a tool of domination.

For instance, under these circumstances, most east European societies, which had been invited to join a free-market economy after the fall of the Berlin Wall and throughout the 1990s, were quickly inundated with the cultural goods of their Western neighbors. They also copied Western lifestyles, with the help of Western media, and celebrated consumerism as a liberation movement with the aid of advertising and Western merchandize – before they realized the consequences of depending on Western capitalism as the road to salvation.

Slovenia is a case in point. Slovene liberalism as a form of nationalism flourished with the aid of mass communication that was culture-specific without being ethnocentric, and with extensive access to foreign media fare, before Western capital acquired media properties, including television stations. The latter now promote mostly American programming at the expense of exploring the potential contributions of a native culture – currently under siege, but maturing and changing in this struggle to assert its own identity and authenticity. At the same time, cultural consumption is not restricted to leisure time. It has become a constant exercise within a social environment that contains a range of cultural stimuli, from the influx of foreign languages – especially English – in public and private discourse, to advertising billboards for imported products, or from exotic consumer goods to Yugo rock.

A living culture is a state of permanent revolution, which reaches for the power of mass communication to sustain its move into a different future and on its own terms, while the notion of imperialism implies a rupture and intrusion for the purpose of redirecting these revolutionary impulses of culture to serve some ulterior goal that is, more often than not, in conflict with the intentions of the host culture.

In the meantime, the quaint images of a small world, if one thinks of McLuhan's global village, or of the persuasive power of a fourth estate, if one considers earlier conceptions of journalism, have reappeared in the guise of a global market and the narratives of worldwide advertising. Indeed, they are the expressions of a new authenticity, if one wants to believe with Thomas Aquinas that truth is the expression of reality.

Mass communication remains a central process for the functioning of cultural imperialism, cultural leveling (at home and abroad), and, in a more general way, of the transformation of culture at a particular historical moment. As a process of representing culture – under economic or political conditions of domination or dependency – mass communication confronts and challenges the cultural resources of a people with the aid of a highly centralized media system that extends the homogenization of culture. The result is a loss of diversity, which applies to the form and content of mass communication and diminishes a native imagination that sustains cultural heterogeneity.

The issue, then, is not so much the undisputed presence of Western media in dependent or developing nations, but their penetration of the respective cultural scenes and their impact on the creation of reality that will shape the lived experience of people, provide new meanings, and replace resistance with complacency, if not acceptance of the status quo. For these efforts, the media also demand larger economic, technical, and social resources than traditional cultural institutions ever did, to employ the instruments of mass communication effectively in the process of incorporation.

In the larger context of cultural imperialism and the charge of its undesirable effects on dependent societies, mass communication has become a politicized concept. This shift constitutes a significant change from social scientific approaches to mass communication in proceedings of cultural colonization or domination, when addressing a politically charged subject from a clearly political perspective becomes unavoidable. Herbert Schiller does so – in the American context – with considerable success. He stimulated discussion of US intervention in the cultural milieu of developing countries during the late 1960s, in particular, and challenged foreign policy goals regarding the deployment of mass communication. His work, although economically determined, places mass communication at the center of concrete political and economic activities and invites a Marxist critique of mass communication, not unlike the work of Dallas Smythe. Together, their efforts focus on the society of the spectacle, to use Guy Debord's phrase, to reveal the commodified process of mass communication in the service of capitalist interests. In a global context, mass communication contributes to the reign of what Michael Hardt and Antonio Negri have called "empire," or an idea of control over social life and human nature, in general, without spatial or temporal boundaries.

The success of this new form of sovereignty depends to a large degree on the deployment of mass communication in the interest of transforming older and more rigidly defined forms of power into an informational economy with fluid boundaries of domination. The notions of empire and mass communication, historically connected since the expansion of the Roman empire, have entered a new partnership in the wake of a post-imperialist period of an expanding global authority.

In this context, the idea of mass communication has undergone an ideological critique that confronts the dominant philosophical foundation of American mass communication theory – a mixture of Pragmatism and liberal pluralism – with a Marxist analysis. The latter represents a philosophy of praxis which is closely linked to an interest in political outcomes. The ensuing project of responding to the real conditions of communication in contemporary society yields two related insights into the place of mass communication: its centrality across the social, economic, political, and cultural spheres of society – and beyond its boundaries – and, therefore, its conspicuousness in what Enzensberger has called the industrialization of the mind. Both insights point to the pervasiveness of mass communication as a social process not only across specific spheres of society, but also across specific technologies (or media) on a global scale. They continue to guide the search for viable explanations in debates over cultural imperialism, specifically, and the question of effects, in general.

Cultural imperialism, however, also faces the potential of culture as an open and receptive environment, which prospers under the impact of external influences and the success of cross-cultural communication. The latter depends on the mode of interpretation and the strength and diversity of mass communication in an international context. Robert Park suggested as early as the late 1930s that the past experience and present temper of an audience are by far the most important conditions for understanding and appreciating information (or news) from abroad, because only cultural traits that are understood are also assimilated, and they are understood only as they are assimilated. He privileges the process of meaning-making by those exposed to mass communication, which plays an important role as a conveyor of cultural traits and a source for interpretive practices.

More generally, the idea of mass communication is drawn into a process of theorizing the role and function of media among philosophical considerations of a democratic existence under new conditions of industrial growth and urbanization.

X

In fact, mass communication in its practical or concrete form has been accompanied by theoretical observations in the larger context of theories of society, especially when media join other institutions, such as those of religion or education, as crucial elements of an intellectual superstructure of society. Thus, theories of mass communication emerged from the discourse of American social sciences during the 1940s, although their beginnings are in the 1920s with the impact of Pragmatism on social thought – and even earlier in Europe, and Germany in particular.

The early writings of German political economists (during the latter part of the nineteenth century) contributed a strong economic bias to considerations of mass communication in the context of traditional ties between politics and business; they focused attention on the real and potential conflict between two major functions of mass communication: public service and private enterprise. But while the German perspective on mass communication emphasized a leader–masses dichotomy in representations of social, political, or cultural developments, an emerging American view revealed a tendency to consider mass communication as a process of representing competing ideas in a classless society; here ideas are available from many sources and offered to the public in a spirit of equality of worth or importance.

This notion resides in Pragmatism, an American philosophy of gradual change, adjustment, and continuity, which celebrates the ideas of community and communication as central to making democracy a workable condition of human existence. It developed at a time when industrialization was sweeping through society and the spirit of evolutionary change was being pushed aside by a revolutionary burst of technological advance that included a new working definition of communication, open to the imagination of private enterprise and safeguarded by constitutional guarantees.

Indeed, Pragmatism recognizes the centrality of communication to a social-philosophical explanation of American society. The significance of the telegraph, railroads, highways, and rivers as means of transportation, and the spread of schools, libraries, and newspapers as institutional sources of knowledge and experience provided the historical background for this theoretical discourse about the central place of communication in modern society. Thus, a generation of philosophers offered visions of communication and inspired a social critique of contemporary developments in mass communication.

Pragmatism as an approach to the study of society also appealed to a new sense of culture that had emerged from the Industrial Revolution with an admiration for democracy as an American experience. That is to say, there was an intention to explore the conditions and meanings under which people interact as enterprising, moral individuals who share in the general desire for improvement. The confrontation between the traditional values and aspirations of a rural community and the consequences of technology and the commercialization of an urban society – extended to the challenge of immigration – offered a context for the development of an American culture. In the wake of major social and economic shifts due to industrialization, urbanization, and education, social thought concentrated on the problems of value and change, tradition and innovation. The emerging spirit of survival, that is, the success of adapting to technological solutions, in turn, symbolized the exemplary strength of the United States for Europeans in their own struggle for a democratic way of life, especially after the experience of World War I.

As most representatives of Western philosophical thought continued to ponder the importance of language and communication, modern exponents began to address the significance of mass communication. It is in this atmosphere of a fast-growing society – committed to liberal democratic values, the importance of freedom of opinion and the opinion-making process, and the role of the media as conveyors of ideas and protectors of various publics and their rights to express themselves – that the idea of mass communication became a major theoretical force. For some it was an extension of previous considerations of communication as a transfer of meanings between individuals that was reminiscent of earlier notions of community. Historical recollection, personal experience, and an idealized understanding of a rural existence in the United States found their way into the search for the "Great Community" and attempted to join ideas of democracy and community, which embraced

60

fraternity, liberty, equality, and free intercommunication among individuals.

Nowadays, references to community have an emotional appeal that is used to imply social, psychological, and geographical proximity as well as a sense of security in the process of incorporation. Since communication is central to the idea of community, its characteristics are reproduced in the process of mass communication to cater to the communicative potential of individuals or groups in society. Consequently, technologies of communication, from highway systems to telephonic traffic and broadcasting networks, reproduce the comforts of physical and psychological proximity, suggest immediacy, and claim intimacy. They are built on an appreciation of communication as a form of social organization. The desire to identify with communal roots also fosters the idea of nation and society and reinforces social and political homogeneity. As a result, individuals may feel closer to each other or to the events of the world, but they are also more isolated in their mediated experiences, since the speed of electronic travel breeds alienation.

Philosophical or theoretical guidance in matters of social communication has been historically divided between a nostalgic view of society as community and a progressive vision of society as empire; both cross ideological boundaries to assert their respective poses. Thus, bourgeois and Marxist aspirations to democratic communication are strikingly similar. They are based on personal commitment, communal needs, and collective investments, although they may differ in their understanding of change, or disagree in their assignment of power. Indeed, the assumptions of a democratic life, steeped in the ideology of free-market capitalism, have remained unchallenged by political forces – such as opposition parties – or social philosophers, including Pragmatists. Instead, criticism and suggestions for change have stayed true to the dominant ideological narrative of the American dream, which upholds communal values and promises a better life.

Thus, the progressive industrialization of the media, from rotary presses to radio sets, television receivers, and computer screens, has been accompanied by an optimistic belief in the betterment of society through improved access to mass communication as each recent wave of new technologies – from cable television to the internet – repeats the promise of accessibility and participation in the democratic process. These waves have consistently translated mass communication performance into speed, beginning in the nineteenth century; it was a time when the French poet Alphonse de Lamartine could exclaim, with reference to the speed of newspaper circulation, that "the book arrives too late." A century later, newspapers were outdistanced by the immediacy of broadcast media, which, in turn yielded to the velocity of computers. Roll film capitulated to digital processes, which rush words and images – made for instant gratification and quick disposal – across the screen and around the globe.

Speed also informs contemporary social and political practices. It is a cultural characteristic whose consequences became most noticeable during the twentieth century with the rapid development of information technologies. Baudrillard once observed that the United States represents the triumph of effect over cause and of instantaneity over time as depth. The result is a lack of contemplation amidst growing opportunities for exploitation and control. Thus, when McLuhan proposes that, with an increasing speed of communication, politics tends to abandon notions of representation or delegation in favor of an immediate involvement of the entire community, he disregards political (or government) intent. For instance, media coverage of war against Iraq demonstrates how the speed of communication aids politics (and the media) in controlling levels of public involvement through propaganda efforts with a predictable ideological slant.

In fact, the principle of instantaneousness dictates the production of information and entertainment and shapes a postmodern understanding of mass communication, in which moment connects to moment without a sense of past or future. Speed replaces reflection, as effect supersedes content and content displaces meaning, in the panopticon of modern media practices. There is no return to contemplation, reasoned judgment, or to a creative pause in the speed of mass communication. Instead, flashing realities are produced without historical consciousness to equip audiences on their travels through social, cultural, and political spaces, gaining fleeting impressions, which are soon reduced to a blurred memory of society. The warning "speed kills" has larger implications for the continuing automation of mass communication and its impact on a new vision of a democratic society, when reasonable demands on time for thoughtful deliberation will characterize the ways of political communication.

Beyond these issues, however, remain unanswered questions about the effects of mass communication, which would not only occupy social scientific inquiries into relations between the media and society for most of the twentieth century, but stimulate a cultural critique of traditional perspectives on mass communication.

XI

The public uses of mass communication technologies, however, has not only confirmed the social and political realities of economic progress, but reinforced attempts to promote the role of mass communication in the conceptualization of democracy. Indeed, the task of combining notions of democracy and communication fell to the social sciences. Social theory, at the time, realizing the tension between reality and possibility – necessary, as Immanuel Kant suggests, for human understanding – transcended the actual world and engaged the imagination. The latter produced insights about communication and a democratic life that dwelt in the realm of pastoral visions of community or in a realization that living with democratic communication as an ideal would remain an eternal challenge. In either case, wanting to live in an ideal world, according to Goethe, always requires treating the impossible as if it were possible.

These developments of mass communication were accompanied by social scientific mass communication research for most of the twentieth century, beginning with earlier sociological observations and ending with a full-fledged academic field of study. The prominence of mass communication studies emanated from the significance of the effect; it is a preoccupation of the reigning institutions with considerable investments in the practices of advertising, public relations, or journalism. The credibility of these efforts rests on the work of the social sciences, whose analysis of mass communication soared to new heights of respectability during the last century. As real life became indistinguishable from the stream of mass-communicated messages, scientific expertise was called upon to identify cause and effect.

This resulted in the production of "mass communication research," a marketable institution that accompanies the production and maintenance of mass communication processes. It appeared within the discourse of the social sciences with a particular understanding of the political and economic importance of social communication, the location of the media in society, and the search for knowledge about mass communication. Based on work in sociology, social psychology, and psychology, in particular – and therefore associated with a traditional institutional apparatus and its disciplinary practices – mass communication research is characterized by a strong bias towards quantitative methods, which are grounded in the guiding principles of positivism or post-positivism.

Such guiding principles ultimately confirmed a social scientific approach that promised detached, value-free, and objective observations. The result was a search for a scientifically knowable world – the lived conditions of a media environment – which is the only world that matters as a legitimate terrain of scientific exploration. Whether such a reality is perfectly (positivism) or imperfectly (post-positivism) captured, however – according to the reigning theories of the past decades – remained part of a struggle, particularly after the 1970s, over the preservation of a dominant discursive practice, which defined the reality of media and communication in terms of invasive technologies and their institutional and collective purposes (or functions). They typically catered to specific social, political, and economic interests and provided the context for the rise of mass communication research as the source of (social) knowledge and (political) power.

For instance, these interests have been institutionalized by a decisive turn from communication to information which coincided with the emergence of cybernetics and a scientific or technical explanation of its significance for society. The notion of an information society, in particular, epitomized already existing social scientific canons of context-free generalization and cause-and-effect explanation and celebrated the potential of prediction and control.

Better yet, the conceptualization of an information society as a logical consequence of technological developments also removed the uncertainty or ambiguity of the older concept (communication) – problematized and applied during an earlier period of progressive thought by members of the Chicago school – and allowed for a scientific construction of social and cultural uses of media technologies. Such an understanding of communication as information was reinforced by the research practices of journalism and mass communication studies and provided the grounding for a instrumentalist perspective on modern communication processes that became part of the reigning ideology of mass communication research.

The increasing need for identification, definition, and explanation of information phenomena contributed to its success and legitimated its claims as a field of inquiry; it also fostered professional ties to commercial and political interests and, therefore, links to the production of knowledge and the exercise of power, as issues of mass communication became socially and politically relevant with rising social problems, ranging from illiteracy to violence, in American society.

In fact, the presence of mass communication research reflects an era of certainty that appeared with the development of a sophisticated social scientific apparatus, including research methodologies. It is the outcome of an accelerated postwar development in science and technology and complements the political-military success of the United States in world affairs. Its reliance on the reign of facts reveals an irresistible bias towards the production of tangible social and political information. The emergence of public opinion polling, with its confidence in methodology and its faith in prediction, reflects the endless possibilities of an applied science that serves the goals of commercial and political interests. It also legitimizes the ahistorical and decontextualized nature of such practices – which focus on information rather than knowledge – to seek solutions in immediate response rather than delayed explanation. Such activities are reproduced prominently in the journalism and advertising of the day as manifestations of social or political events. They perpetuate a theory of society whose notions of truth and reality are imminently discoverable versions of the dominant ideology.

Consequently, mass communication as a social phenomenon has become a prominent research topic with references to social, cultural, political, and economic practices that embrace the idea of communication as information. At issue are typically questions of compliance with the pronouncements of the reigning social, economic, and political practices – and therefore control of information and information flows couched in terms of media effects – rather than issues regarding the absence of or resistance to such effects. To paraphrase Antonio Gramsci, the hegemonic struggle involves captivating, not capturing, the masses, with a media environment that will always distract from the real conditions of society. This culture of distraction becomes the territory of administrative mass communication research.

Thus, accessibility of media technologies and standardization of content – or what Theodor Adorno and Max Horkheimer called the industrialization of culture – are the foundations of an information society that exists with the expenditure of a minimum of communicative effort or competence. Their combined effects – important for military and economic purposes during periods of external and internal competition and conflict – constitute the tangible evidence of production and consumption practices. They provide a measure of mass communication in society that speaks to the distribution of power and influence. Under these conditions, progress in mass communication research is the accumulation of knowledge based on perfecting prediction and control of media and information phenomena.

Even today, the attempt to understand the notion of media effects and their consequences through experimentation and manipulation (of variables), in particular, reflects a central concern of the field as it continues to relate to social, commercial, and political issues of society. It also constitutes a major preoccupation with methodological issues at the expense of theorizing communication or developing alternative models of media applications. The lingering popularity of mass communication research as a legitimate social scientific enterprise has helped strengthen the institutional claims of the media industry on leadership and control in society.

By the end of the 1970s the social scientific gaze of the observer enforced a regime of decontextualization or randomization that raised questions about the relevance of inquiries whose exclusionary nature provoked the possibility of new paradigms and encouraged critical voices from within the field. Thus, as the result of a theoretical position that produces knowledge by accretion, relies on verification of *a priori* hypotheses, and seeks a generalizability of its findings, mass communication research joined the ranks of a social science tradition whose bas ic belief structure has come in for close scrutiny and outright critique by a growing number of alternative perspectives. After all, social scientific constructs, and the idea of mass communication specifically, are still cultural inventions and, therefore, subject to revision and change.

The social and political conditions of communication in the world – beyond the parochialism of US mass communication research – have produced a creative and potentially useful atmosphere of critical introspection, encouraged by emancipatory movements and supported by historically conscious reconsiderations of knowledge about communication. As a discursive shift produces a new understanding of communication, it reveals alternative perspectives by introducing a number of useful options to rethink the notion of communication as information. Thus, it is no accident that during the latter part of the 1980s, in particular, refocusing on the "critical" in communication became widespread, while mass communication as a field of study looked for new ways of understanding its own history and meeting the challenges to its traditional paradigm.

In addition, accessibility to the more recent cultural discourse in Europe – including a sustained critique of capitalism – also introduced alternative ways of thinking about communication. These new perspectives were particularly effective, because they addressed directly the traditional concerns of mass communication research related to the role and function of media in society, while their theoretical possibilities contained the potential for a major paradigm shift.

For instance, the previous notion of information society underwent an ideological critique when communication was reintroduced as a viable, if complex, concept of human practice. In fact, the idea of communication related again to human agency and the emancipatory struggle of the individual, and political considerations of communication and media encouraged practical responses to concrete problems. The result was a discursive shift that provided opportunities for alternative ways of conceptualizing society, the public sphere, and the nature of democratic practice itself, based on an understanding of a historically grounded reality of institutions and practices that could be grasped, interrogated, and reconstructed through a dialectical process. It reflected a materialist-realist position and suggested the importance of material differences in terms of the conditions of communication, or the place of the media at a given historical moment.

Furthermore, Marxism and Cultural Studies introduced an ideological dimension to the study of communication; they recognized the importance of power and confirmed the significance of human agency for communicative practices. Both insisted that the goals of their respective inquiries were the critique and transformation of specific social, political, or economic conditions for the purposes of social and political change, specifically, and emancipation, generally. Thus, they insisted on the role of advocacy and were apt to embrace (social or political) activism grounded in the changing nature of historical knowledge and its potential for different explanations of a contemporary way of life. Ideologies, like language, are symbolic systems that are produced by a public discourse – in or exclusive of certain facts or fictions – and in the service of specific reconstructions of reality. Ideology, language, and mass communication are also linked to form an articulated belief system that finds its expression in the work of media and support from a community (of believers) which resists change.

Under these conditions, the acquisition of knowledge and the emancipatory goals of critical communication studies are defined by the prospects of change and reconstruction, as ideas become obsolete and are overruled by new insights and practices. In fact, a critical communication theory renews itself as it confronts different conditions and is propelled into different historical situations.

As a result of these developments, mass communication research has been challenged to abandon its secure ideological location to become part of the inquiry by joining an agenda that reflects the activist (and often confrontational) stance of critical communication inquiry. Such a position suggests that facts cannot be separated from the domain of values, that the relationship of meaning and language to culture is central to constituting reality, that the interpretive nature of culture and communication precludes a fixed or final truth, that the relations between representation and reality are political, that thought is mediated by historically grounded power relations, and that privilege and oppression in society are reproduced, although perhaps unwittingly, by traditional research practices.

Coming up against an alternative critical discourse – produced by a convergence of writings identified with the critical theory of Max Horkheimer, Theodor Adorno, Herbert Marcuse, and Erich Fromm, the later work of Jürgen Habermas, the contributions to cultural studies of Raymond Williams and Stuart Hall, and specific references to the works of Louis Althusser, Antonio Gramsci, and Michel Foucault, in particular – mass communication research faces a formidable challenge to its traditional position. Because together these writings produce a new and different type of knowledge, one that focuses on notions of culture, empowers the individual, and addresses the consequences of an industrialization of the mind to expose relations of power in the process of communication and provide a forceful critique of cultural practices.

Critical communication studies reproduces such theoretical considerations and constructs research agendas that reflect the need for alternative readings of communication and media. Thus, a Marxian tradition open to the critical currents of postmodern social theories promises a postmodernized practice which extends the critique of culture and communication beyond deconstructing the dominant discourse of mass communication research. Its responsibility in the context of a shifting discourse of communication and media studies is twofold: to identify contradictions and negations located in the objective narratives of empirical mass communication research, while exposing its ideological nature, and to connect theoretical considerations of communication and the media with the specifics of everyday experiences.

The first task involves the review and analysis of the decontextualized construction of mass communication as a social process and the adoption of its definitions across social and political formations. Such a review reveals the discursive practices of mass communication research over a considerable period and suggests its limitations as a socially and politically responsive approach to an emancipatory social strategy involving communication and media. The second task addresses a systematic, historically grounded, and politically informed examination of the nature of contemporary social communication. But most significantly, perhaps, both tasks require active participation and suggest social and political commitment. to a concrete involvement in emancipatory causes that lead to transformations in communication and media with the disclosure of contemporary practices, discourses, and representations of culture.

When postmodernism arrived in the United States amidst an ongoing critique of mass communication research, and culture in general, it was met with ambivalence or suspicion, although its arguments helped deconstruct the received notion of mass communication.

Paradigm shifts in the context of academic work are the result of complex social, political, and cultural developments that enable ideas to rise and take hold of the imagination of individuals in their own struggle against a dominant professional ideology. The decentering of mass communication research occurred under such circumstances – aided by the influence of modernist and postmodernist European ideas related to notions of culture, ideology, and power and the increasing relevance of language (and the production of meaning) in the study of social formations – in addition to a rapidly shifting terrain of communication studies away from narrow conceptualizations of media and towards the inclusive category of culture.

The resulting practice of theory and research reflects the workings of a critical consciousness on issues related to the privileged and authoritative knowledge of mass communication research and contributes to a blending of the humanities and social sciences as a major intellectual project of recent years. Contemporary writings about communication and culture explore these extensions and offer evidence of mass communication research as a blurred genre among signs of a more radical break with tradition.

Decentering mass communication research, however, has not resulted in terminating universal or general claims to authoritative knowledge of communication and media. It is equally clear that mass communication research has been challenged by intellectually and ideologically formidable alternatives, and that the process of demystification proceeds with the help of socially and politically conscious examinations of communicative practices and the articulation of emancipatory ideas through an expanding literature that engages the field in a critique of culture and commodification in a democratic society.

Finally, critical communication studies as an institutional framework may help promote the importance of self-reflection as a first step in a process of reconstructing relations of domination by offering theoretical insights, providing interpretive, qualitative research strategies, and encouraging resistance with the goal of implementing a democratic vision of communication and media. Such a task can only succeed as a socially conscious practice, however, after critical communication studies exposes the relations of power in the production of knowledge and the dissemination of information. Challenging the instrumental rationality of an administrative or corporate discourse reconfirms its own role as an historical agent of change.

In the meantime, however, the constitutionally grounded relations between mass communication and democracy continue to face a series of problems, which are related to historical issues of societal growth, media uses, and individual engagement in the process of democratization.

XII

The centrality of communication in definitions of democracy has been undisputed since the passage of the First Amendment to the United States Constitution and the subsequent inclusion, following Supreme Court interpretations, of other forms of mass communication (besides the press) during the earlier part of the twentieth century. Similar developments occurred in other democratic societies, especially throughout Europe, where freedom of the press became the cornerstone of democratic thought about the future of society after the end of World War II.

But the later history of mass communication is more often than not a history of struggling with reasons for protecting narrow political and economic interests, and with issues of ownership and access to the means of communication that support democratic practices which benefit society as a whole. Thus, the undisputed centrality of mass communication has been a recurring concern throughout its history, whenever special interests own and control the media.

Beginning with the bourgeois revolution against aristocratic rule, means of mass communication have been effectively applied in hegemonic struggles and subsequently controlled by those in power. There has never been an outright sharing of space or time, or free access to major media outlets for all relevant political operatives in a democratic society. Instead, opposition has either been marginalized and confined to its own process of mass communication, or coopted and integrated into expressions of the dominant ideology. In addition, of course, advanced industrial capitalism produced commercial interests that have gained significant control over the media to succeed in industrializing the manufacture and dissemination of information and entertainment. Their powerful hold on the media, including their ideological formation, has brought political interests under their control and defined the democratic landscape.

The understandable fear of media effects has been widespread, beginning with the paternalistic conceptualization of the "fourth estate" as a public watchdog and ending, most recently in the United States, with the invention of "public journalism" and its articulation of media obligations to society in response to much older insights into corporate uses of the power of mass communication over people.

These concerns have typically been expressed in cautions regarding media uses which have accompanied the rise of mass communication, starting with printed matter and accelerating with the introduction of visual and electronic media. Such an unease has focused on traditionally contested areas of freedom of mass communication, including social and moral control over public expression. The latter issues have not significantly changed over the centuries, although the degree of public tolerance undoubtedly has. For instance, fear for the moral health of movie-going children, dismay over violence on the television screen, and consternation over exposure to pornography on the internet or in recordings have prompted campaigns against media practices – with mixed results.

Likewise, books continue to be banned from public libraries for similar reasons.

Industry responses have mostly been political gestures that typically result in voluntary censorship, rating systems for film and television, or controls on computers, but rarely discourage producers of mass communication – even after a religious, conservative public has continued to pursue its agenda for the moral and physical well-being of young adults, and society in general. On the other hand, sponsors have regularly interfered in programming since the time when television programs were controlled by single companies; for instance, after public protests and sufficient publicity, depictions of violence have led advertisers to pulling commercials off the air.

A democratic vision of society must address the more fundamental and politically important relationship between mass communication and democracy, however, beyond these border skirmishes on the outskirts of mass communication issues. American democracy, specifically, relies on mass communication to reproduce a feeling of familiarity, and an atmosphere of mutual trust and shared knowledge to promote consent and create conformity rather than empowerment. A renewed battle for democratic communication, often anticipated but never undertaken, must be conducted to help clarify notions of participation, access, and control of the means of mass communication while insisting on freedom of the press as a universal right rather than a particular property right.

At the center of this struggle resides the issue of mass communication as a finite or limited societal resource with potential benefits for all of society, that is, equality of opportunity for participation in the process of mass communication, not as subject, but as citizen. While the former symbolizes the condition of inequality, the latter personalizes a sense of a rationalized social and political equality between media and individual, for instance.

Not unlike natural resources – such as air, water, or oil – media, too, are limited in their availability. Their numbers are determined by economic constraints – loss of profitability in the case of too many competitors, overpricing and shrinking markets – or physical limitations – a shortage of broadcast frequencies or a scarcity of forests for paper production. Also, the performance of self-defined tasks, such as informing and entertaining society, may be restricted by the limited availability of intellectual labor or creative talent. In any case, what remains is a well-founded need for widespread participation, particularly among the working class, whose expectations for inclusionary politics continue to grow with increased literacy and education, and despite lacking material prosperity.

Since democracy is identified with capitalism (in the United States), the democratization of mass communication is predominantly an economic issue that focuses on the power of media corporations and their influence on the planning and execution of mass communication strategies in pursuit of private profit and at the expense of public interests. Their creation of consumer demand is backed by advertising revenues and demonstrates the workings of market relationships that control the mass communication process. The United States is a business, operating under a business ideology.

A democratic vision of mass communication, on the other hand, is based on establishing more humane conditions of existence, which include a liberation from the influence of privileged commercial interests. Change demands a set of different actors, such as cooperatives, community owners, public-interest control, or employee ownership of the means of mass communication, for a more balanced relationship than the one that is based on a predominantly corporate media economy. The question of public participation hinges on an ideology of participation, or on a public commitment to the task of creating and maintaining an environment for democratic communication.

Participation in the process of mass communication is based on the principle of access. Its understanding begins with the issue of competence and includes the acquisition of literacy, communication skills, levels of education, and expert knowledge; it continues with questions of controlling the production of content and the uses of dissemination technologies. It also involves the notion of economic affordability, which begins with the cost of (higher) education and ends with the price of a quality newspaper or magazine – including marginalized publications – as a source of continuing education.

The latter is an important consideration, because lack of education affects communicative competence, and lack of access to an informed discourse leads to social or political blindness; it may even breed resentment. When access is blocked by pricing policies, people tend to make do with whatever is affordable and accessible, but television and radio are no substitute for print media, including books. CNN does not replace the *New York Times*, for instance, and free shoppers are no match for local newspapers; yet, economically deprived individuals are forced to rely on their only access to inferior information sources. Access to the internet is not universal – it also involves investment in technology and transmission fees – and is plagued by economic issues similar to conventional media uses. In addition, computers – and the internet – are environments of individual activities, which require intellectual abilities in support of curiosity and a desire to know.

As people become acquainted with the one-dimensionality of information or entertainment that characterizes cable news programming – but is equally visible across networks and local stations, and in many local newspapers – they are rendered speechless. Incapable of articulating their own distinctive (political) positions, because this state of mass communication coopts the language of the oppressed – or the masses – which is always poor, monotonous, and immediate, according to Roland Barthes, considerable segments of the population experience mass communication as a process of confinement rather than liberation.

A successful mode of participation calls upon the complex of social, cultural, political, and economic determinants of a democratic existence, and therefore moves beyond traditionally held views. These began perhaps with Adam Smith, Karl Marx, or later social prophets in the United States such as William Graham Sumner, who thought that the individual is economically determined and that economic needs must be the controlling condition. After all, a passion for material well-being was the foundation of what Charles Peirce wanted to call the "Economical Century."

These views furnished a rationale for constructing audiences economically (as paying customers) and considering mass communication as a process of integrating individuals into a consumption cycle. There was no further concern for their general welfare, including the consequences of their citizenship in a democratic society, when they appeared as "the masses" in the literature of the day. Walt Whitman referred critically in his *Democratic Vistas* to the relentless pace of economic development when he wrote that the "New World democracy" remained an almost complete failure in its social aspects, but also in its grand religious, moral, literary, and esthetic results, regardless of its success in uplifting the masses, in material developments, and in a highly deceptive superficial popular intellectuality.

This "superficial popular intellectuality" was the result of mass communication, which later on produced "infotainment" and distraction by trivia; it was also a consequence of cultural deterioration, as mass culture critics charge, when the authority of the unqualified rules expressions of mass communication. Later criticism echoes these concerns, blaming corporate ownership for changing expectations of professional standards and returning, albeit implicitly, to the economic determinants of mass communication.

It is a devotion to business that characterized nineteenth-century American life, and mass communication reproduces its atmosphere in structure and content. Structurally, it represents the efforts of private ownership, aligned with other business interests, that forge an identity of media property as commercial investment rather than civic responsibility. Its content is a reminder of merchandizing and reproduces an adscititious vocabulary, which includes words such as industry, business, commercialism, or capitalism. These are the symbols of a new materialism that emerged from the Industrial Revolution and became the ideological markers of mass communication in its industrial phase. The latter describes the developing relationship between democracy and mass communication since the start of the twentieth century. It replaces the democratic phase of mass communication, which began when democratic goals of equality and participation were pursued under the guidance of bourgeois thought.

The struggle for freedom spread throughout the rest of society and provided change, encouraged by a feeling of inclusiveness that came with the practice of communication. Thus, the fight for justice and equality (during the nineteenth century) was fought with means of mass communication that were available and accessible to those struggling to be heard. For instance, party newspapers, pamphlets, and campaign posters were widely used, giving individuals a voice and a sense of belonging. Democracy was experienced in the act of communication, as John Dewey describes it in *The Public and its Problems*.

But the time had passed and the proximity between community and communication vanished, since *Gemeinschaft* had already turned to *Gesellschaft* when society entered the twentieth century. The world had become too complex for most individuals, as Walter Lippmann warned in *Public Opinion*, and he became increasingly pessimistic about the future of democracy, starting with the incompetent individual. Since then, the history of mass communication has been the history of a deteriorating relationship between ideals of democracy and understandings of communication.

The enormous technological advances in mass communication that came with industrial growth – for example the invention of the telephone, electric light, linotype, phonograph, photography, and movies, but also the automobile and the airplane – produced paradoxical results. While this development enhanced and enlarged the production and dissemination of culture, it eliminated most people from the process of social communication as it had removed them earlier from production and transformed them into consumers (also of mass communication). For example, while the typewriter, the telephone, or the camera invite participation and allow the unrestricted expression of ideas, the industrialization of film, radio, or television reduced individuals to audiences.

This permanent shift from individuals as producers to consumers of the societal narrative has never been reversed, regardless of the late arrival of the computer, whose built-in freedom of choice is being threatened by government regulation. Thus, the idea of a nurturing and protective press, described by Karl Marx, the journalist – who uses the term *Volkspresse* – which functions neither as an authoritative instrument of elitist control, nor as an exclusive publication for and by a specific class, but as a public sphere that accommodates the voice of the people with its own tolerance for dissent, has never been realized. Neither has Walter Benjamin's suggestion that in a truly socialist society every newspaper reader is also a writer or reporter. Nor the ad-free newspaper (*PM*) of Ralph Ingersoll in New York, or the commercial-free television programs in Europe or the United States. Although these notions remain an ideal premise for participatory social communication, they remain historical reminders of attempts to break with the industrial models of mass communication.

Moreover, media content – from news to entertainment – was adjusted to serve a growing market by providing more access to information and entertainment as goods or services, instead of contributing to the development of more democratic practices with opportunities for emancipation. Intellectual freedom is never the issue as long as journalists or other creative workers remain subservient to media ownership, while the latter insist on being identified with democratic practices and the idea of press freedom.

Indeed, press freedom evolves for all practical purposes into an institutional protection of ownership and property, rather than into a protection of journalists or writers, for instance, against the special interests of proprietors. The continued use of the notion of a fourth estate, initially a British creation, serves to underline the paternalistic, authoritative role of the media in contemporary society and begs the question (again): in whose interests do media operate, and what is the role of journalists, or, for that matter, of readers?

The dilemma of contemporary journalism, frequently addressed in economic terms and focused on the changing nature of media ownership, is the end-product of a preferred cultural construction of journalists. Such a construction is a historical phenomenon which has its roots in the making of American journalism and the relationship between the institution of the press and the individual contribution of labor. In fact, the idea of journalism as a cultural practice has undergone significant definitional changes related to shifting notions of work, including technological advances in the workplace, and the predicament of a volatile market economy as media interests merged with the politics of mass society.

The press has rarely been a facilitator of intellectual labor free from a business-oriented paternalism that directs journalists in their work. The social and political consequences of a hegemonic approach to professionalism are the demise of traditional notions of journalistic practices and the rise of corporate power and control over the contemporary role and function of journalists, the manner of mass communication, and the purposes of the media in general.

Such conclusions also have serious consequences for society and the relationship between information, knowledge, and democracy.

They not only suggest a new system of gathering and distributing information, but, more fundamentally, a new authority for defining the nature and type of information that provides the foundation of social and political decision-making, and a new partisanship that embraces the patrons of commerce and industry; in this sense, it offers a new understanding of democracy as private enterprise rather than public endeavor, when extent and quality of information, including its specificity and accessibility, depend more on the social, economic, or political needs of commerce and industry than on the requirements or needs of an informed public.

When journalism has served society in the role of information broker, it has been strengthened by its history and fortified by the perpetuation of its myth, which rests on a belief in the availability of truth, the objectivity of facts, and the need for public disclosure, to create and sustain the idea of journalism as a necessary institution for a democratic way of life. Although journalists have played a key role in the advancement of their own cultural and political legacy since the last century, they have been frequently coopted and deceived by media ownership in its own attempts to obtain the confidence of large audiences for political and economic gains.

Journalists have adapted to the uses of mass communication technologies, as did others in media positions, including printers and linotype operators, with some trepidation. Yet, there was never any real doubt about the benefits of technological progress for the democratic foundations of society, which is strengthened by the presence of an increasingly sophisticated and far-reaching media system that would produce and disseminate information or entertainment faster, cheaper, and more widely.

Since technology is not autonomous but develops within the context of economic, social, and political institutions, the growing technical sophistication of the means of mass communication is evidence of (political) choices that pit the advancement of mass communication against the decline of social interaction, for instance when television invaded the home. This development not only raised issues of social control, loss of privacy, and lack of social communication, but also posed questions about the transfer of creative knowledge from journalists or writers to corporations and their technicians. Also, technologies of mass communication, while overcoming geographical distance, generate a distancing of the subject, who becomes alienated in the absence of an irreducible, dialogical face-to-face situation. In other words, not mass communication technology as such, but its organization, control, and creative application remain major problems in capitalist societies.

Mass communication is an urban phenomenon that responds to consumer demand. The media offer entertainment for the masses, or prepare information for those with communicative competence; they sell space and time to others who want to be heard. All of this has less to do with a need for a democratic discourse, and more with a desire to advertise products or services. Thus, with the identification of their patterns of consumption, the participatory element of mass communication has been reduced to what people want; the result is media fare that remains highly sensitive to shifts between need and desire. In fact, mass communication also implies a manufactured commonality among people that is based on a leveling of taste cultures and an undoing of ideological differences. The goal is to deliver an aura of compliance that promises tranquility while reinforcing the dominant ideological order in society.

The exception to these developments – which may be found mostly outside the United States – has been the more recent history of public media, such as broadcasting, in Japan and most of western Europe after World War II. In these cases, the process of electronic mass communication became a public responsibility as ownership fell into the hands of citizens whose representatives acted independently with mandates that had no ties to commerce or politics – or at least in some instances and at the beginning of this development. The lesson of the last half-century, however, has been that public ownership alone does not guarantee a more egalitarian or democratic system of mass communication. What is also needed is political control and a built-in accountability without commercial participation. Nevertheless, the result has been the creation of a pluralistic system of media ownership in many European societies, which shifted to include a two-tier system of broadcasting when the state capitulated after political and commercial pressure for private ownership became too powerful to resist in the early 1990s.

The idea that the state is responsible for conditions that ensure not just the liberty of individuals, but their ability to realize their own potential – a feature of liberalism – has resulted in the liberation from slavery, despotism, and other ills brought about later by industrial interests. Given the centrality of communication in any democratic society, the contemporary task must include liberation from ignorance, from lack of communicative competence, and from institutions, like mass media, that are oppressive or non-responsive to issues of participation and democratic communication. In fact, John Dewey described this emancipatory condition once, when he argued that genuine freedom is intellectual, because it resides in trained thought and the ability to look at matters objectively. Given the fact that human fulfillment is found in communication and shared experience, opportunities must be created within the mass communication process to accommodate individual empowerment.

The need for change is a condition of existence that prevails in contemporary societies; only a free, knowledgeable, and communicatively competent individual will be able to address options and suggest new directions in the liberating atmosphere of a participatory democracy. The development of mass communication, nonetheless, shows a steady decline of the relevance and even importance of its offerings for the lives of people whose alienation from society has affected democratic practices. John Dewey's definition of radicalism as a perception of need for drastic change led him to conclude that any liberalism which is not also radicalism is irrelevant and doomed. It also reflects his impatience. The time for introducing radical change is still at hand – not on the part of the culture industry, with predictable outcomes, but through the intellectual engagement and political imagination of individuals who see the means of mass communication as a public trust.

XIII

Initially however, the cause of mass communication as a constructive element in an ideology of progress was helped by a celebration of the relationship between technology and democracy. It was an expression of confidence in the merger of private enterprise and public interest and cast aside doubts – if there were any – about its consequences for societal communication. Indeed, the mass media were quickly swept up in a technological revolution that, during the early twentieth century, distinguished the United States from Europe as a place where democratic practice meant access to and use of the concrete manifestations of progress: automobiles, freeways, skyscrapers, the suburbs, and electricity for everyone. In addition, mass-circulation newspapers and picture magazines, Hollywood movies, and radio transmissions spread familiarity and raised expectations.

There was knowledge about rather than knowledge of society – as Robert Park distinguishes the process of knowing the world – with its own dynamic of defining a nation in terms of cultural and political homogeneity long before fast-food chains and public personalities would introduce new forms of authenticity. The latter emphasized the uniqueness of the shared experience, when communication exhausted itself in the act of consumption. It was a ready-made culture that embraced ready-made information to serve mass consumption, not unlike the widespread use of the Sears Roebuck catalog (or the Bible, for that matter) to spread ready-made ideologies of material (and spiritual) consumption around nineteenth-century rural America.

Since then, mass communication has become the expression of an ideology of commercialism that dominates society and dictates the rules of communicative encounters within the public sphere. Participants in the discourse of consumption are the affluent, economically stronger classes of society. There are no material or cultural goods designed for the oppressed, who become communicatively marginalized in their societal role. There is also no communication link – or media effort – to understand their culture and assist them in overcoming a predicament that has been caused by society.

In fact, new technologies of mass communication have not lowered but raised the barriers between classes, with higher costs and higher intellectual demands. They have also destroyed traditional rhythms of work and leisure, which include ways of obtaining and disseminating information that have been replaced by the media. In the process, civil society is being divided and identified by significantly different relations to mass communication.

On one hand, a smaller segment of society – the upper classes – is intimately tied to the processing of information – and the creation of entertainment – which derives from expert sources, like quality newspapers, specialized journals or magazines, highbrow broadcasts, and serious film, besides theatrical performances and classical concerts. Together, these sources of intellectual and creative insight constitute a comprehensive and complex foundation for advancing practical knowledge and participating in the affairs of the state. Their communicative strategies include the perpetuation of a language of domination that finds its expression in the performance of mass communication. One is reminded of Roland Barthes's observation about the bourgeois oppressor, who conserves the world through myths and in a language that aims at eternalizing.

On the other hand, the majority of individuals – or the lower classes – are denied access to these resources, both for economic reasons and also because of a serious lack of bourgeois competencies, ranging from literacy and levels of education to social or political engagement in a critical response to a mediated reality. Confounded by exposure to various forms of mass communication, such as television or radio, these individuals are without any real opportunity for a comparative approach to other sources of information or entertainment. This is not a matter of taste, or taste cultures, but a question of choice, and not only in the interest of participating in the discourse of a bourgeois society, but also for the sake of strengthening class identity.

Reliance on media organizations for specialized, technical knowledge by an educated elite has become the foundation of a new patronage system that privileges a sophisticated generation within the bourgeoisie, which benefits from technologizing mass communication. The resulting information gap continues to produce cultural, social, and political divisions that reinforce a two-class society of information-rich and information-poor individuals, with dire consequences for the survival of democracy. Paradoxically, mass communication, originally conceived of as an instrument of social control in some of its forms, is rapidly changing into a privilege of social, political, and cultural elites, capable of making public judgments because they can be informed. Mass communication, in this case, becomes communal and intimate again; its growing exclusivity reflects an idea of democratic communication that stimulated its rise as a political symbol and an expression of democratic practice in the first place.

But the demise of mass communication as an element of democratic practices within national boundaries has been successfully obscured by a growing interest in the politics of globalization. These (political) interests have seized on collective experiences with the process and effect of global communication during half a century of commercially generating and disseminating ideologically charged information and entertainment throughout the world. From Hollywood film to CNN television, mass communication enterprise produces global audiences and meets global commitments in a historical process of cultural leveling that replaces authentic feelings of belonging to the local with a false sense of belonging to the world. Absorbed by the process of mass communication, individuals search for their identity among the social or commercial constructions of self. But, reduced to spectators and defined as audience, they become alienated from their own existence while engaging in rituals of cultural consumption.

It has been a long time since Harold Innis described the relationship between empire and communication or Herbert Schiller warned about the consequences of an American empire of mass communications. But both realized – albeit in different ways – the effectiveness of a system of mass communication that emanates from centers of political and commercial power. The outcome is not only technological control of media systems, but also a rigorous reorientation of communication practices, from language uses to viewing or listening habits, while disregarding systematically the need to protect and nurture the autonomy of cultural differences. Moreover, as we have seen, the politics of mass communication threaten the sovereignty of democratic societies by inviting individuals to a discourse they cannot share and into a reality they cannot understand.

Thus, ample supplies of mass communication products raise expectations – regarding economic and political participation, for instance – that cannot be fulfilled. The resulting frustrations – even when not turned into violence and destruction – have long-term consequences, not only for those caught without clues between the cruel facts of an ordinary life and the propitious myths of mass communication, but also for others who already know that only the privileged live in fictions and survive. For them participation turns into an alienating process of consumption with only limited options for escaping the pervasiveness of political, economic, and cultural agendas of mass communication. In other words, the freedom of an individual to be misled, seduced, and eventually incorporated, turns quickly into an unfreedom that comes with burying local autonomy, language, and customs under a flow of ideologically determined information and entertainment.

While the effectiveness of mass communication in the globalization of the mind is undisputed, however – as is the usefulness of the media in its support – success still depends on domination and control. Thus, the call for freedom of the media has become a rallying cry of those whose politics continue to prepare the ground for a re-colonialization of the world. They constitute an alliance of those in control of the means of communication, including a new elite, whose interests in reshaping the world know no social solidarity or respect for democratic institutions. Instead, they perpetuate the myths of free markets and the vision of a free world with the help of mass communication to reinforce their own vision of an open territory for the expansion of their economic and financial assets. This remains the most blatant example so far of the abuse of mass communication against public interest and necessity and its collapse as a means of spreading and fortifying the idea of democracy.

In other words, we have come a long way from a time when, in the early years of the twentieth century, bourgeois idealism fought for the rights of a free press to strengthen the idea of democracy and for notions of joining technology and democracy for the benefit of a new democratic order.

Not unlike the histories of other enabling technologies – from nuclear science to biogenetics – mass communication technologies share the risk of after-effects for the life of a democracy. The history of mass communication technology has been a history of consolidation, concentration, and centralization. It began in modern times with the availability of superior technologies in the days of American radio, when networks supplanted local programming. Culture became a domestic product, and the presence of local talent gave way to the packaging of fame and the rise of national stars. This decisive shift from the political concerns and cultural specificities of a William Allan White to the national agenda of broadcasting networks, and later to the geopolitical focus of a Rupert Murdoch, for instance – had extraordinary consequences for the political and cultural life of society.

The creation of national (and international) markets and the production of national (and international) television broadcast audiences for commercial purposes has solidified the power of economic interests over the means of mass communication. These interests are confirmed (and strengthened) by subsequent political decisions to eliminate regulatory hurdles, for instance, and streamline control over broadcast licenses. The politics of deregulation has validated the sharp turn to a strategy of persuasion that has redirected media attention (including print) from information to entertainment. This shift has affected the quality of news and, more fundamentally, the nature of journalism; it has become a business whose function is the satisfaction of needs for diversion rather than for information.

The consequences for a democratic society are catastrophic, however, when journalism falls under the purview of an entertainment industry, and the task of engaging in surveillance and an independent critique of political practices becomes the responsibility of gag writers and comedians. The reduction of mass communication to a process of responding to what people want is the result of free-market policies that privilege the intent of commerce to promote and sell, while ignoring the complicated task required of the media in the interest of advancing the cause of a democratic society. Mass communication has been permanently installed in a system of marketing the industrialization of civil society. The survival of the democratic practices of mass communication – if it is possible at all – calls for diversity of ownership and purpose of operations as well as of content, and requires reinforcement and protection of the (political) information function of the media.

The loss of this perspective, with its cultural roots in the history of mass communication, and journalism in particular, may have brought about an artistic critique that surfaces in movies from *Citizen Kane* to *Network*, but without much critical response from

86

industry, politics, or even the general public. Critical attacks on the media are most frequently met with indifference, such as that of the post-World War II Commission on Freedom of the Press report mentioned earlier, which dealt intelligently and thoroughly with media performance and expectations for a democratic system of mass communication. Also, unlike other governments, such as those of Canada or the United Kingdom, that of the United States has never established an official press (or media) commission to report on the state of mass communication in a democratic society at a time of commercial threats to the integrity of the means of mass communication as an instrument of political discourse. Instead, economic interests have determined relations between politics and media policies.

These interests are not necessarily identified solely with specific branches of the media industry, but more typically – and increasingly – represent broader and more powerful organizations, such as General Electric or Walt Disney, with far-reaching business agendas. Media property is often maintained for revenue purposes, and with no vested interest in the quality of journalism or the role of mass communication in a democracy – but with the added advantage of providing an outlet for products and an instrument for persuasion and manipulation.

But even organizations which have only media holdings, such as Gannett or Murdoch, are first and foremost for-profit corporations whose strategies are aimed less at living up to the principles of democratic mass communication than at expanding revenue growth. More importantly, however, media ownership vis-à-vis political interests, located in political parties, representatives, or government, represents in itself considerable political power focused on the execution of commercial agendas and on political decisions regarding regulatory issues pertaining to mass communication.

The influence and control of economic interests is not restricted to the information function of the media, however, but extends over the cultural realm, in general, as it shapes the form and content of the popular culture industry. The latter is based on exploiting mass appeal and mass behavior and dedicated to the merchandizing function of mass communication, in which it absorbs and exhausts the cultural resources of society. There is no sustainable creative career outside the culture industry, which defines genius by inclusion on bestseller lists and record charts, or television rating sheets. Innovation and popular creative effort, especially of oppositional voices outside the industry, are frequently coopted and incorporated, and thus politically neutralized and commercially exploited.

The success of media organizations with their strategies of producing popular realities is frequently attributed to individual choice. In fact – as Herbert Gans suggests – taste cultures in a democratic society rely on what people choose; they cannot exist without them. Under current conditions of mass communication in the hands of commercial interests, however, taste cultures (whether high or low) are manufactured and compromise specific individual (or group) standards; individual choice is restricted to availability rather than specificity of taste. In other words, availability represents the range of experience and becomes the universe of choice, because there is no other option in the world of mass communication.

Despite the best intentions, regulatory foresight, or ethical strictures – dominant claims, couched in terms of national interest or free-market principles, often prevail, with questionable, if not disastrous, results for the public interest. Since the question is not whether the media are manipulated or not, but who manipulates them, a reasonable solution is to make everyone a manipulator – according to Enzensberger, who believes in the revolutionary potential of the media.

Today's employment of communication technologies in support of oligarchic media systems simulates public trust while ending a traditional understanding of democracy that appreciates mass communication as a shared democratic practice. In fact, mass communication reinforces the specter of a mass society (and its totalitarian features) with centralizing features that reach across the social, cultural, and political domains of society.

Democracy – by its very nature – is always a collective work in progress, since it embraces a commitment to change. Problems arise in political systems that insist on perpetuating their past (if not stagnant) versions of democracy on the strength of historical clout or traditional practices. Thus, the United States has been reluctant to experiment with (or change) political institutions or their ways, while other societies in Europe or Asia – whose experience of democratic systems of government is much shorter — seem quite willing to amend their ideological and material manifestations of democracy, from voting rights for foreign labor to media owner- ship. Once persuaded by the desirability of change, the process of renegotiating the meaning of democracy requires political flexibil- ity and, more specifically, a commitment to mass communication as a mode of public participation.

2

Mass Communication and the Meaning of Self in Society

The uses of mass communication in the lives of individuals are a major social and political concern; indeed, the media are important sources of knowledge for understanding the world as a practical reality beyond the customary dreams of mass communication as a collaborative force in the making of a participatory democracy. Instead, the process of mass communication emerges as a constructive force, limited however, by its own interests and prejudices as well as by the degree of intellectual or creative power among individuals as spectators, whose successful intervention in the flow of mass communication introduces ideologically diverse world views. If language is, as Martin Heidegger argues, the dimension in which human life moves, then mass communication is its technological extension, which supplies a working vision of reality that is historically grounded in its own narrative. To be sure, such a reality is always a representation of knowledge about the world, constructed under specific social, economic, or political conditions, employed for effect, and shared at a concrete historical moment for specific purposes by the dominant order.

I

Mass communication in its modern version is an utterly American idea. It is conceived to secure the prospect of social control with a focus on the process of socialization, the method of mediation, and the circumstances under which effects can be achieved. In addition, it is useful, fast, and efficient, but also versatile, typically operating in the present, and open to social scientific scrutiny. As such it reflects the American experience of a world that is knowable and, for that reason, conquerable.

Mass communication also belongs to the vocabulary of the American century, like freedom and democracy, where it constitutes the most popular synonym for the current conditions of modernity, joined by terms like mass culture, mass society, or mass market and buttressed by the principles of mass production and mass consumption. It is a twentieth-century concept with obscure origins and applied beyond academic circles by a public awakening to the consequences of a technology-driven modern existence. The idea of mass communication certainly attracted public interest before the celebrated alliance between democracy and technology showed signs of exhaustion, and the novelty of urban thrills and suburban bliss had turned into an alienating experience for a growing number of individuals.

When notions of wealth rather than welfare direct the long march of society towards capitalism, casualties are left in its path, according to keen observers of twentieth-century society. For instance, Erich Fromm's or David Riesman's classic laments include the complicity of mass communication in the conditioning of modern society. Ideologically compatible in its predominant forms, and therefore rarely subversive, mass communication is seen to help create consensus or compliance through diversion. The initial duality of generating accounts of reality involving the media and expert narratives, for example governmental or scientific authorities, is being collapsed into a single system of generating public or social knowledge through an economically inspired collaboration of shared political interests. The latter range from the widespread use of public relations materials emanating from business and government to a centralization of information sources.

This essay, in particular, shifts from institutional manifestations of mass communication to its reception by individuals, or from the external circumstances of social or political conditions to internal matters of shaping an understanding of reality in the minds of individuals. After all, the encounter with mass communication is also a private or personal experience that involves ways of receiving information and knowledge for the construction, adaptation, or conversion of meaning.

Since the beginning of the twentieth century, almost three generations have grown up in a mass-mediated environment, which defines their lifeworld and provides the intellectual and emotional context for an understanding of their social and political existence. The resulting relationship between the individual and mass communication raises questions about the nature of reality, freedom, and control over the prospects for an authentic life; it also problematizes the discovery of the self in the process of mass communication, since its permanent presence in people's daily lives has masked the potential for social communication successfully and in a totalizing manner. Thus, when the spoken word yields to transcription and preservation as text, and speech becomes not only frozen but disembodied in the flow of mass communication, information is lost and knowledge cannot be recovered. Colin Cherry once talked about worlds in a wink, and he meant the potential richness of face-to-face encounters.

Moreover, mass communication – as it turns out – may be a deceptive practice, whose truth claims are not a matter of knowledge and interest, but of faith in the act of representation itself. Seductive in its simplicity, artful in its construction, and even convenient in its ability to control through force of habit and persuasion, mass communication is the choice of the powerful with access to the world of media. The idea that freedom of the press exists for those who own it is a classic comment, not only on the prerogatives of ownership, but also on the mediation of the social or political order under which people live and die.

The sense of communication, which is the foundation of an authentic existence, has changed to include the presence of the media, reflecting the institutional forces of society and resulting in a rapidly disappearing private realm. Communication is no longer communion, as John Dewey would have had us believe earlier in the twentieth century, but rather responsiveness to sophisticated strategies of economic and political interests in the public realm. These strategies rely confidently on the lifelong process of socialization by media institutions. For instance, with the rise of science and technology the reproduction of society by mass communication has resulted in a mystification of the methods of liberation; the search for individual freedom remains confined within the process of mass communication, where the image of progress resists surrender to the real conditions of social communication.

The limits of progress were described some time ago by Erich Fromm, among others, in an apt portrayal of individuals in a capitalistic society, who see themselves engaged in an effort to define the meaning of their own being in the world. Their private lives repeat the monotonous pace of work, constituting the calamitous oscillation of a modern existence. Indeed, people read the same newspaper, listen to the same radio programs, and watch the same movies regardless of their social standing or intelligence. The unquestioned rhythm of their lives consists of production, consumption, and enjoyment. Not much has changed since 1955, when Fromm considered these conditions, except that television, and lately computers and computer or video games, have been added to the standardized media fare. The latter occupy even more time in the daily lives of individuals, providing additional opportunities for a lockstep existence and reinforcing the opportunities for social and political control.

Technologies of communication, driven to perfection by the march of science, competition, and profitability, rule definitions of society – or the details of a social and political being – and replace the very idea of communication with a form of participation as consumption that relies on the desire to satisfy real or false needs. Not knowledge but information has become the fashionable commodity of the time, not the *littérateur* but the journalist dispenses wisdom in the public arena, it is not the public that speaks, but the (self-styled or media-appointed) expert who advises. In fact, genres are obscured when information is marketed as knowledge and journalism claims the role of philosophy. There are critical differences, not only of substance, that make the acquisition of knowledge a fundamental aspect of human existence; they grow out of curiosity, experience, and the desire to widen and secure the boundaries of understanding the world. Knowledge is a product of human communication; it involves the exchange of ideas, a lasting commitment to dialogue, and a willingness to learn from cooperation. It is also a human achievement, which relies on the ability to communicate and to share experiences.

Since communication is a process, or a way of life, as Raymond Williams suggests, it bears the essence of being human. It is also a resplendent course through mind and soul, inclusive of facts and fictions, open to the world of the other, and to risk and failure for the sake of experience. Indeed, communication is the experience of life, which means it is also based on the human qualities of intimacy, voice, and understanding that come with a shared existence. Mass communication, on the other hand, reinvents these essential traits, constructs substitute happenings, and fashions itself as human agency. In fact, it claims the total individual while it is the essence of inauthenticity, and its inescapable centralizing function promotes generalization, denies diversity, rejects individuality, and, in the process, silences the sound of communication.

Mass communication cannot exist with the ambiguity of subjects or events; it also tends to categorize the extraordinary as the normal and prefers the present to the past, or immediacy to history. Its construction of current events, however ideologically tainted, becomes the object of historical inquiry, where it rises once more to the status of "fact" or "reality," despite misgivings about the course of journalism through time and place, for instance, and the production of information as knowledge by special interests. The influence of mass communication reaches across the impact of the day's news to affect considerations of people and events beyond the grasp of their contemporaries.

II

Knowledge and concern regarding the effects of mass communication – individually and collectively – have been around for as long as the media have made a significant difference in the life of society. They have been based on the myth of writing – the pen is mightier than the sword – and on its operationalization through propaganda efforts that have activated media at various points in history, particularly when social or political change has been feared or

94

welcomed. Mass communication serves to solidify people – or as Harold Lasswell suggests more specifically, propaganda is "this new hammer and anvil of social solidarity."

Suspicions about the effectiveness of mass communication have systematically increased with every introduction of new media, especially during the twentieth century, when new forms of mass communication dramatically changed the landscape of societal communication. For instance, the arrival of the movies provoked public reactions against the explicit treatment of topics ranging from adultery or homosexuality to narcotics; comic books experienced hostile reaction to portrayals of violence; television programming reinvigorated these debates with concerns over the effects on children; and the internet is now raising questions regarding universal access to hate messages or pornographic websites. Often politically or socially motivated, these reactions are based on moral claims and supported by social scientific research that is frequently much more cautious in its conclusions than the rhetoric of specific publics – including religious organizations, conservative civic groups, or campaigning politicians.

More generally, the public significance of mass communication research is primarily a function of media interest in (dependable) self-knowledge and has coincided with a greater reliance on advertising revenues with the change of basic media economics. Readership studies, in particular, became the early providers of reliable facts and figures about audiences, followed by the desire of the media industry to test the effectiveness of advertisements. Joseph Klapper's summary of effects studies in the United States in the late 1950s made it quite clear that there were conditions under which mass communication may be powerful – a reminder of earlier fears of propaganda. Although it became more politically convenient perhaps, for media representatives (and some academics) to suggest, with Klapper, and, thus to alleviate suspicions regarding media practices in society, that mass communication does not ordinarily serve as a necessary and sufficient cause of audience effects.

Beyond surveys, social scientific research has applied content analysis and conducted laboratory experiments to probe mass communication effects, while remaining atheoretical and ahistorical throughout its development into a major source of public insight into the workings of mass communication. It has also mostly succeeded in the form of what Paul Lazarsfeld once called administrative research – or what mass communication does – rather than critical research, which questions the role of mass communication in society. The former benefits commercial (or political) organizations in their quest to gain public approval, or to reinforce positive dispositions towards products or services. Indeed, the consumer constitutes the major target of administrative mass communication research. Its (marketable) product is the description of the "effect," on audience behaviors or attitudes towards goods or services.

The preoccupation with the impact of mass communication derives from an everyday presence of media saturated with social values – which are ideologically determined by such terms as propaganda, public opinion, or mass media, for that matter, as well as, in general, by the process of labeling. Mass communication research also recognizes the potential of change – from the behaviors, attitudes, and opinions of individuals to the ideological positions of social formations – associated with media practices in society. Although effects may have been greatly exaggerated in the past – by those involved in research or in political or social struggles – it remains likely that mass communication, as the only means of identifying and assessing the significance of daily events, is an increasingly potent means of bringing about modification or change; for that reason alone, mass communication is the preferred territory of effects research.

In this endeavor, the individual as a representative of the consuming masses becomes an important object of study at a time when the circulation of commercial or ideological messages sustains the media, beginning with newspaper coverage and continuing through subsequent developments to the pivotal role of television. The image of the isolated individual, which emerges from earlier sociological considerations of modern society as an impersonal and alienating environment in which mass persuasion is an accomplished media practice, begins to change, however, with the rediscovery of the primary group and the impact of interpersonal communication on the structured nature of an audience.

In addition, experimental work – prominent since the World War II and the controlled studies of Carl Hovland and others – has provided additional insights into the workings of mass communication on an individual's ideas or behavior. The findings from experimental work – while offering increasingly complex answers to questions about the potential of mass communication that seem to support a powerful effects paradigm – are in conflict with surveys or panel studies of audiences, which yield a far less powerful model of mass communication. The individual emerges from those studies equipped with agency and personal power. Quite predictably then, the apparent discrepancies within mass communication research lead to a selective use of empirical findings for political or commercial purposes.

Considerations of mass communication effects on individuals range from the "magic bullet theory" – consistent with sociological and psychological theories of the time – which anticipates the immediate, uniform, and direct effect of messages on every audience member, to a more sophisticated understanding of selective influences based on the specifics of the personal and social attributes of individuals, including social differentiation and social relationships. Thus, the discovery of the effects of informed personal relationships through the movement of information – from media to informed individuals and to others with less direct media contacts – revitalizes the notion of individual power, and the role of opinion formers, through personal influence, which restores confidence in the importance of face-to-face communication.

The pursuit of these ideas by mass communication research has led to the realization that effects may not be immediate or direct, but subtle, indirect, and with long-term consequences for culture and society. Those consequences, whether real or anticipated, relate to the role of mass communication in the process of socialization, that is, in reinforcing continuity and predictability in the life of society, and in equipping individuals to conform to the social order. Communication is a crucial element in the socialization of the individual, since it stimulates participation in the shared reality of everyday life. Such a reality is created and disseminated through the process of mass communication and with the help of media organizations, and their efforts to describe the dominant norms, roles, and practices and provide a language of expectations that becomes a predictable text for individual (or social) action.

Mass communication is closely involved in the social construction of meaning; this was discussed in the 1920s by Walter Lippmann in his *Public Opinion*, but it reappeared in traditional mass communication research, particularly in cultivation theory and agenda–setting. Lippmann suggested that individuals act on "pictures in their heads" that have been constructed by the media (the press) and contribute to their understanding of reality. Meanings are shaped by the politics of media and become realities when they are exposed through the "unique perspective" of television coverage, for instance. Also, a mediated reality may influence conduct, since television cultivates people's beliefs. And then there is the power of the press (in political reporting, for instance) to set agendas for the public discussion of specific issues, thus creating the meaning of events and their importance for public life.

Most recently, however, cultural studies has focused on meaning and meaning-making as a culturally shared practice, which differentiates and empowers individuals and enables interaction within the larger environment of mass communication practices. This intervention of cultural studies in the traditional approach to media studies, and mass communication research in particular, signals a turn to a critical cultural perspective which discards models of direct influence and implements an approach that addresses the ideological role of mass communication. It also reintroduces the individual as a credible and forceful participant in the shaping of the social environment. Cultural studies locates mass communication practices within " a complex expressive totality," that is, in human practice, and provides and selectively constructs social knowledge and a complex, acknowledged order, according to Stuart Hall. The individual appears in this setting as resisting the power of media by engaging in "preferred readings" of mass communication that produce a view of the intellectually interested, empowered individual, who is able to circumvent the intent of mass communication through "excorporation."

This view provides the basis for identifying cultural studies with strengthening and perpetuating democratic practices. Beyond the idea of culture as an appropriate site for explaining mass communication lies the interest in a social and political critique of society with an emphasis on questions of ideology, power, and domination in the context of mass communication, which is the context of public life in a media environment. In fact, the activist tradition with its roots in British cultural studies continues to offer an alternative vision of mass communication research not as administrative re- search in the interest of commerce or politics, but as a form of social criticism that enables the liberation of the individual from the cold embrace of mass society theories. In this sense, it is a theoretical approach that encourages the individual to become active and to make a difference in opposing oppressive manifestations of mass communication that threaten democratic forms of social practice.

It is also worth remembering in these paradigmatic shifts to a critical position how little was accomplished by traditional social scientific studies of mass communication during the last century. Much of what is known today about the role and function of the media, for instance – or the notion of effects, in particular, and the process of mass communication in society in general – has been understood (and discussed) for centuries by generations of intellec- tuals, whose creative insights quickly revealed the workings of any (new) cultural phenomenon in their midst, from pre-Socratic rhetorical scholarship to nineteenth-century thought about the political economy of the German press, for example. In the mean- time, social scientific analyses have steadily accumulated to bolster an already considerable body of findings concerning the impact of mass communication without producing a new theoretical under- standing of its workings in society. Consequently, when it comes to theorizing media and society, the social scientific study of mass communication remains complementary or additional at best, and fragmented or without context at worst.

III

Individual encounters with the manufacture of reality reveal the themes or stereotypes of media practices that fashion the experi- ence of everyday life in an environment that looks and sounds familiar enough without being the "real thing"; the latter remains the personal experience of being in the world with others. The dif- ferences between a mass-mediated reality and the reality of personal experiences are significant in terms of substance and complexity of social, political, or economic issues and their solutions as well as in terms of time, speed, or duration. Nevertheless, the media play a significant role in the lives of individuals as a source of insights into a complex contemporary existence.

As a result, the American way of life is a product of mass communication, through a variety of commercial media, as is its ideologically determined dissemination around the world. The media rely on the selection and presentation of information and entertainment that compel individuals to conceive of their existence in specific ways, especially since the repetitiveness of an endless stream of mass communication creates consistency and conformity of a composite view of the world, which is confirmed when advertising and news or entertainment join in the continuous celebration of the "good life."

It is no surprise, then, that the mass–mediated world (of the United States) is an affluent state of affairs, based on a representation of pervasively high standards of living, which materialize on screen and in print in the form of new cars or appliances, smart housing, or luxurious clothing in well-appointed surroundings that show no signs of use, no marks of poverty or crime, in uncompromisingly safe neighborhoods. It is an impeccable, predominantly middle–class environment, in which mass–produced consumer goods take on the appearance of designer products not only to meet expectations of uniqueness, but to confirm and reinforce one's place in the community of spenders. These material conditions are joined by ideational accounts of a middle-class ideology with its traditional renditions of nation, community, religion, and freedom and responsibility. After all, the mass–mediated realities of pleasant work, desirable professions, and carefree living – supported by an ideal social or political ideology – also guarantee more opportunities for spending time and money in a leisurely way.

This imagery is developed with remarkable consistency across genres (such as news, entertainment, or advertising) in a process of mass communication that is designed to address a middle-class society – or those who claim to belong to it – without much thought of those whose economic capital has no bearing on projected consumption levels and whose political power is negligible.

In this sense, it is the picture of a classless society that invites audiences to identify with specific depictions of the ideological and material conditions of existence. The latter contain the prospects of a life in which social problems are personalized – that is, where alcoholism, drug abuse, AIDS infection, divorce, or child abuse conveniently happen to the other, thus creating a psychological distance that facilitates a vicarious coexistence with social ills. In other words, a concrete approach, with the help of real faces, clearly defines social problems as individual issues with individualized solutions – for the other – which will not significantly distract from the playful diversions of a media reality that is designed to encourage identification with the dominant system. As a result, increasing crime rates, or violence in general, are recast by news organizations as morality plays to address the fears of the unaffected and warn about the social (or economic) consequences of deviance for the status quo.

Existing social or economic differences are also worked into a visualization of "good" or "bad," especially in film and television, that makes for drama and teaches lessons that reinforce conformity. Thus, "bad" individuals do drugs and commit crimes, although the public rarely learns about the complex social or economic reasons for antisocial behavior. Misfits maim or kill to serve selfish goals; they don't succeed, but will most likely be punished by fate – another term for the forces of "good," which engage in justifiable violence to subdue ill will and address disturbances in society. The lesson, while aiming to be entertaining in its frequently excessive violence on either side of "bad" or "good," is always the same: crime does not pay and the guilty will always receive their justified punishment.

Like personal disasters, social or political problems are posed and solved within a short period of time. Mass communication must offer assurances of a socially or politically satisfactory response and dispense instant gratification. Again, personification allows for the removal of problems without the need to explore their complexity; it is a principle that has also surfaced in politics, if one rethinks the war rhetoric regarding Afghanistan or Iraq. Echoed and intensified by (popular) media with no sustained critical engagement, journalism, as an allegedly independent source of insights, relies on stereotyping and themes of evil and violence that entertain rather than

101

inform. Since evil is always punished swiftly, war becomes the only recourse open to the pure and virtuous in a two-dimensional mass-mediated reality of good and evil. More recently, however, the customary delivery of audiences to the commercial sponsor has been extended to include the government (in the United States), and politics in general, as the ultimate sponsor with regulatory and legislative powers to bring to bear on media ownership. The official construction of an "embedded" journalism in the process of hostile military engagements in Iraq, for instance, is a powerful example of the merger of government conduct and media interests.

Mass communication enhances the social environment with its elaborate production of a personal sphere; for instance, penetrating social (or political) media realities and privileging youth, while catering mostly to white Anglo-Saxon audiences, ideas about love and devotion, marriage and family life, including divorce, become the mainstay of media fare that reaches beyond entertainment. Expressed in the form of stories, dramatized in episodes of "reality" television, or even featured in news programs, these accounts – not unlike newspaper or magazine advice columns – have a moral to be eagerly shared with the masses.

Yet the complex problems of the "real" social environment – such as class, gender, or race relations, politics, or work – rarely inform the mass-mediated reality for individuals, whose actual experience makes them expert witnesses of the production of falsehood or the simple omission of facts. Thus, working-class life rarely makes it into the media, either as a dramatic performance or a news item; when the homeless disappear from city streets, they also leave the site of the media and are abandoned – again. Issues of gender equality are trivialized, if portrayed at all, while race relations are pushed into the background as they relate to economic and political issues, stereotyping, and blatant racism – the political biographies of contemporary politicians are a case in point.

The mediated realities of politics and work reflect middle-class concerns without exploring the potential of political action or workplace reforms, for instance. Instead, they are celebrated as traditional sites of American enterprise, especially on prime-time television, while news accounts signal an awareness of political or corporate corruption and slave labor practices of major US com-

102

panies abroad. In the case of both social problems and criminal behavior, media treatment is frequently ahistorical and often short-lived; mass communication rarely employs its potential for a sustained, long-term commitment to a particular cause or issue. Its memory, locked away in archives, rarely surfaces to add an explanatory historical dimension to the respective coverage, and when it does, its interpretive capacity is overshadowed by its documentary character.

Representatives of an administrative class – such as doctors, lawyers, police detectives, or military officers – crowd the media reality as exemplars of a ruling social or political power elite. They are the idols of authority, to paraphrase Leo Lowenthal, who have come to join the idols of consumption to perform in the spectacle of mass communication, vying for the attention of audiences, whose own ambitions to occupy the subject position of their idols, however, remain unfulfilled. They are also representations of a new heroism, which is identified with the collective power of societal institutions rather than with the symbols of the rugged individualism that characterized earlier manifestations, for example the cowboy-hero in Western movies.

Representations of working-class lives, on the other hand, remain confined to mostly inconsequential episodes in sit-com environments, or are reduced to comic figures; foreigners are treated with suspicion and exist as stereotypes in their media appearances. In fact, nationality and ethnic origin dictate their fate as friends or foes from countries that are mere labels on a world map that has not been comprehended for years.

The geographic reality of mass communication is a reality of unraveling events, when maps, weather forecasts, and on-the-spot reports contribute to breaking news accounts that fail to provide knowledge about an otherwise nonexistent cultural or historical context. Since Vietnam, other regions, such as Kuwait, Kosovo, Bosnia, Afghanistan, and Iraq provide more recent media lessons in geography designed to explain an American presence abroad rather than the existence of another, possibly ancient, culture elsewhere in the world. After all, the mass-mediated reality is an American product that appeals to an American construction of the world, which is rooted in American feelings of personal freedom and beliefs in material security. More generally, the relentless spread of imagery throughout the world reinforces an American perspective: for example, the popularity of CNN news clips elsewhere suggests that the world is seen through American eyes.

In the search for personal identity, ethnocentric realities produced by mass communication, for instance, turn the more intimate idea of love into an American film and television creation. For instance, love, not unlike sports, becomes the active and engaging pursuit of, if not the hunt for, an object of desire, which meets traditional expectations of romantic love in terms of age, race, and gender. It happens mostly to young, racially compatible, heterosexual individuals, whose physical attraction is carefully portrayed; there is no sex, but suggestions of passion, which seize up after marriage, when an amicable – even slightly hostile or resentful – relationship prevails. The home becomes the focus of a marital life in which wives rather than husbands become effective leaders and problem-solvers with great energy and efficiency. Children are not born, they just appear, as Gilbert Seldes observed years ago in *The Great Audience*, and fatherhood becomes just another challenge and a source of conflict in dramatic terms. Work is a natural condition, albeit without protection against arbitrary management decisions; union membership is rarely an issue and neither are labor–management relations. They remain, like so much else concerning the real conditions of work, unexposed, and become at best material for context or background.

But crises at home or at work drive the drama and suggest that (married) life consists of confronting an unending series of trivial predicaments. Yet relationships endure, faith in each other prevails, and threats of separation or divorce are successfully dismissed. If not, breakup or dissolution are the consequence of major (social) problems, such as alcoholism or promiscuity, rather than intellectual (or sexual) incompatibility. The stability of marriage as a social institution becomes an ideologically charged issue and the reason for the dramatic struggles that unfold weekly in the media realities of family life.

Finally, while heroism provides opportunities for strengthening the myth of individualism, its manifestation resides more frequently in institutional contexts – such as the police or the military. Yet it remains a favorite topic of coverage across the media spectrum, in news reports and fictional accounts alike. There are always heroes in the manufactured reality of an American life, whose message never varies: the cause is worth the sacrifice, and the cause is frequently the defense of traditional institutions, such as nation, family, or religion. These are noble causes which generate feelings of patriotism and serving a greater purpose, regardless of the real motivation. It is idealism in action, designed to address the alienated and isolated individual with optimism about belonging to a community of heroes, and being American.

In the mass-mediated reality nobody dies alone, or is abandoned to a fate of utter resignation; on the contrary, there are always solutions, material security, and emotional support. The idea of community, with all of its implications, comes to mind and rules the day of television-watching or magazine-reading. Despite a myriad of social, economic, and political problems, there is youthful optimism and a naive belief in the ability of the individual to endure and survive in order to eventually be materially independent before riding off into the sunset or living a complete life in the isolation of a retirement village in Florida or Arizona, for instance.

In the reality of American television programs an uneasy juxtaposition of black and white neighborhoods, generations, or families creates competition for time slots rather than for mutual respect and understanding. It is a divisiveness that may well be based on commercial grounds rather than on racial policies, but it becomes political when it happens, and it suggests again the dominance of economic interests over social or cultural issues.

Mass communication suggests that life is good in a capitalist society until the very end; this idea is rarely challenged by those most affected by the social and economic conditions, because they cannot afford to listen – for economic reasons – to dissenting intellectual (or political) voices from a wider reading of thoroughly informed and enlightened critiques of the dominant order. Because people are economically restricted in their choice of media, they must live in the one-dimensional world of commercial television, where fact and fiction have merged. More recently a calm discourse has been replaced by screaming (not talking) heads in what is still another form of collapsing boundaries between the sound of commercial and noncommercial messages. Television in the twenty-first century seems to have rediscovered the power of the voice rather than perfected the power of the word as it privileges volume over substance.

As a source of social knowledge and a representation of life and work in society, mass communication provides more caricatures of a concrete existence than thoughtful consideration; the latter occurs in literature and (mostly foreign) films, or documentary projects of noncommercial media, where creative insights and intellectual power address the challenges of being in the world. Yet these opportunities are not widely exploited, or even known, since the mass appeal of light and undemanding media fare prevails among program producers.

IV

The pervasive visual extensions of contemporary mass communication invite closer consideration of the image as a representation of the self. Especially since the individual is invented and confirmed by mass communication in the roles of citizen, neighbor, sexual object, or human being, the respective attributes of these roles are constructed and reinforced through processes of recognition and identification that involve media events and personalities. The latter, in particular, are carefully produced to project ideologically correct versions of the self in society, beginning with a cultural awareness of the body.

It is a topic that is hardly new, as Michel Foucault reminds us (in the first volume of *The History of Sexuality*) about the body as an object of knowledge and a significant element in the relations of power, at least since the seventeenth century. Since then, the body has become a signifier of political correctness and power in its multiple reproductions throughout media narratives. Moreover, and analogous to Jacques Lacan's observation about the mirror phase of children, mass communication, and television in particular, contributes to the recognition (or misrecognition) and identification of the mirror-image of the social self. The process of looking turns into self-awareness among the constituents of the social world; it draws attention to the ego ideal and its presence in media narratives, which typically impersonate the ordinary and, thus, return to the familiar for purposes of identification, beyond class, gender, race, or ethnicity, to the specifics of the body itself.

For instance, over time the idealized representation of the body has shifted from ostentatious obesity as a signifier of wealth or material well-being – until the violation of one's own limits turns into the dreaded stigma of the social outcast – to the notoriety of anorexia or bulimia as faddish symbols of denial – and therefore power. Weight as a sign of social substance, or status, turns into anti-social (or medical/pathological) evidence with considerable ramifications for the quality of one's social standing. This is a particularly relevant development for women, as they meet the unforgiving rules of a glamorous life among the material symbols of status and success. Most important among them is an acquired thinness to suggest social (or political) mobility and confirmation of personal progress or liberation. The body becomes the medium for a message of achievement or failure.

Mass communication in all of its forms promotes the modern shape of male and female bodies, most blatantly, however, through advertising, and particularly in the reproduction of fetishized parts – legs, breasts, or lips – which suggest attainability of form through the process of consumption. These parts have been rendered to perfection by various imaging techniques; their social significance is validated and strengthened by representations of television and movie personalities, who not only fortify the notion of reality, but reinforce conforming behavior, especially among women and young girls, as they seek their identities in the public sphere. Thus, while celebrities sell products – often in a testimonial style – they also sell their bodies as explicit statements of beauty (in terms of shape and size) and expressions of aesthetic norms that represent politically desirable and socially acceptable standards (in terms of whiteness or color).

The consequences of compliance may hold a promise of sexual power, marked by the moment of surrender, but mass communication also illuminates the strategies of the beautiful en route to attaining social status. Appearance – from posture, clothing, or the accouterments of luxury to attitude or mindset – is a form of ornamentation in its physical and psychological states which makes the body culturally visible and locates the personality in time and space. After all, the ego is a mental projection of the body surface, according to Sigmund Freud. It is a surface constituted by size, shape, and dress, which is projected through mass communication into the world with an aura of purity that flows from the practice of packaging – and a preoccupation with hygiene – as manifestations of social or cultural development. The packaging of the self is a response to contemporary conditions, in which appearance signals social standing, or lifestyle, efficiently and effectively for a fast-moving society, while the ordinary remains unattractive and therefore marginalized. There is distraction, however, when capitalism introduces the fleeting notion of glamour, which is based on the discourse of fashion and on a collaboration with mass communication to reproduce the fanciful articulation of corporeality. Indeed, glamour is a surface phenomenon of industrial societies; it belongs to the marketing efforts of public relations or advertising, where it is produced to undermine ordinary tastes and create desires for transformation and change.

Mass communication enforces the conditions of subjectivity, which are articulated by appearance and located in categorical requirements for the body and in the specifics of clothing. Mass communication also provides the clues for defining social status, with references to the cost or value of objects or events whose exclusivity marks the boundary between self and others. Hence, appearance suggests power and ensures presence as a form of authority; it is regulated by fashion, which, like mass communication, is about imitation and demarcation, as Georg Simmel reminds us regarding its social adaptation and its uses within specific social classes. It is also a form of social control, which releases the individual from personal responsibility.

The cultural visibility of the body is greatly improved by the use of visual media. Looking through the eye of the camera is a dominant way of perceiving reality, and the art of photography, specifically, has come to control the reality of the body. Film and television enhance this visual technology of the gaze, not only by adding movement to the visual narrative, but by perfecting the visibility of the self by the self for purposes of recognition and identification.

While the self as a social structure – and an object to itself – arises in social experience through communication and remains distinct from the body – as George Herbert Mead suggests – mass communication collapses this distinction and identifies the self with the body. By dramatizing the material conditions of being, mass communication succeeds in extending the idea of the body as individual identity to its audiences, whose attention is fixed on the external dimensions of the respective media narratives. More generally, mass communication promotes awareness and knowledge of the body; the latter serves the production of what Foucault has called the docile bodies of the modern state by introducing for public consumption versions of the perfect body that lead to conformity. In the process, considerable time and effort are spent on a public discourse about the body, health, and good looks, which offers models of compliance and promises happiness through inclusion.

The enabling power of photographic technologies has helped stage personal changes (of the body), while confirming the centrality of the image in the (re)production of the self as body. For instance, an obsession with thinness has conquered the world of design, from cars to Coca Cola bottles; it focuses on the female body as the prototype of the liberated shape that fires the imagination of a health-conscious generation with its mania for fitness and bodily perfection. Supported by the credibility of medical observations regarding obesity and mental health – and siding with the social power of medical knowledge – mass communication takes advantage of a pervasively negative self-consciousness and perpetuates the craving for less – which means spending more – in advertising campaigns for diet foods, diet pills, and exercise equipment in ways that augment the visibility of the perfect body in popular culture. In doing so, mass communication also constructs an environment of fear and anticipation that shapes the vision of the body as an object of desire and a material expression of personal failure or success. Consequently, and in the accelerating process of reduction, an ideal body is the one that no longer materially exists, as Stuart Ewen once remarked.

The image consciousness of modern society is a result of mass communication and its relentless exploitation of people's narcissistic tendencies. The ability of photography to preserve the contours of the face as a record of the past, for instance, not only relates to the Western tradition of portraiture, but its almost instant popularity – which is a reminder of the democratization of the visual image – enables, if not encourages, frequent encounters with a reflection of the self. Thus, aided by the availability of still or video cameras, the pleasure of posing for the camera and the power of role-playing in staged events may be of limited, familial importance until they are explored by commercial interests in portrayals of an ordinary life. The latter becomes exotic and offers entertainment that often feeds on the flaws of the other and, therefore, avoids the banality of the ordinary self.

Image consciousness becomes a new form of self-knowledge that surrenders authenticity to celebrate the spectacle of the celebrity as a source of insights into the personal. Indeed, mass communication succeeds as a tool of separation, when images as commodities separate the experience of privacy from their producers, who are isolated from their own images in the process of mass communication.

V

Mass communication participates in the discovery of the social world as a politically relevant source of information and a means of constructing identities; it is a locus of a discourse which produces the objects of public knowledge – as Foucault suggests. The construction of meaning – or meaningful practice – is unthinkable without the process of mass communication, which produces realities that give meaning to subjects and practices. The importance, in this case, is the realization that knowledge of the world derives from the culturally specific discourse of mass communication at a concrete historical moment. From it flows power and the potential of knowledge to become effective – or true – in its construction of reality. Thus, mass communication becomes powerful in its discursive practices through which it influences the state of public knowledge.

As the self traditionally develops in the company of the other and in the context of face-to-face communication in a community setting, mass communication intervenes with a reproduction of the social experience and a construction of identity that replaces mutual recognition with an assignment of roles and norms. The other-directedness, which David Riesman describes as a characteristic of modernity, and which depends on the presence of others, engages the discourse of mass communication for recognition and definition of personal identity. Mass communication reproduces a sense of community with references to a familiar symbolic environment, which appeals to personal needs for securing one's identity – or creating a new one – and protecting its fragility through extended exposure to repetitive representations of roles, gender models, or conditions of existence. Thus, the notion of standing within a social order, which characterizes the traditional idea of identity, is replaced by standing in an imagined and mediated community of social or political stereotypes. Communication, which involves participation in the other and which requires the appearance of the other in the self, as George Herbert Mead reminds us, is replaced by mass communication, which involves an enlistment of the individual as audience for purposes of identification with products and ideas.

The concomitant routines of mediating reality – which are always ideologically informed – result in an understanding of social relations, culture, and the social and political world in an atmosphere in which conversation is replaced by instruction, and human companionship by an institutional presence. Human agency, in this case, involves a developing awareness of a mediated object world through which self-awareness is formed. In addition, the industrial construction of the other (which is always a fabrication) – and the concurrent realization of the self – which combine the need for efficiency with a desire for maximum effect, are typically directed at audiences as individuals, while signaling the decentering of the personal with mass appeals for identification with objects of mass production. Indeed, Alexis de Tocqueville's "democratic individualism" disappears in a process of mass communication, in which selfhood emerges from a collective exposure to mediated realities that are void of discursive possibilities, that is, when conversation has ceased to be the source of individual self-constitution, and collective identities arise out of compliance rather than opposition and resistance.

However, the narratives of mass communication – and of film or television, specifically – reinforce the desire for identity by connecting with traditional, if not archaic, forms of identity, such as names, images, or roles, and by confirming their external origins, or the fact that identity is attributed rather than inherent in the subject. In other words, mass communication assures the individual of being perceived or recognized by addressing these desires for identity in a performative practice that shifts subjectivity into the realm of economic considerations, where identity, or the sense of belonging, is tied to consumption or collective notions of political participation that range from ideas of "audience" or "consumer" to "people" or "nation," respectively. The ultimate goal remains an identity of (consumerist) consensus through an assignment of subjective identity in the process of mass communication that offers ideologically consistent choices – in the realm of popular culture – to fit the need for conformity and acquiescence.

Beyond its distinctive role in the search for individual identity, mass communication serves the process of identification of social, political, and economic actors and their respective environments. Knowledge about the concrete as well as the imagined world is crucial not only for understanding one's own identity – and its social or political consequences – but also for recognizing the (constructed or fabricated) condition of the other as friend, neighbor, rival, or enemy. It is the mapping of a cultural landscape of needs and desires, of ideas and practices, that makes mass communication indispensable, and therefore also ambiguous as a dependable process of identification. Yet most individuals must rely on traditional media for the surveillance of the environment, the characterization of essential social and political actors, and the chronicling of practices or events.

Mass communication engages in the process of identification as a way of reporting or describing the details of an event with claims that range from accuracy and fairness to perfection and truth, often disregarding subjective biases or institutional ideologies that must influence the reconstruction of reality. This process refers to the life experience of individuals, including the past world of media representations, in order to solicit understanding or cooperation. After all, the social order depends on shared meanings. The result is an

112

authored perspective on the world that reflects the construction of a (journalistic) narrative in a concrete historical situation for the specific purposes of informing, entertaining, or even persuading an audience.

The use of stereotypes – described by Walter Lippmann in the 1920s as preceding the use of reason – constitutes one way of labeling people or events that offers instantaneous identification with a minimum of effort. It also ensures recognition and provides a shortcut to an ideologically charged assessment of facts or figures, whose proof is implied by the use of labels, such as "communism," or, most recently, "terrorism," which carry a host of historically determined meanings. Stereotyping is often used by news organizations to create oppositions, like "them" and "us" (in criminal or conflictual cases), which help accentuate the drama; but they also equate a current concept – or its future treatments – permanently with a particular ideological position.

In addition, television, and the time-conscious world of broadcast journalism in particular, is a stereotyped world of mechanical responses which either imply conditions or contain statements that reflect politically or culturally specific ways of seeing people or events. Lippmann's suggestion that perspective, background, and dimension of action are frozen in the stereotype fits modern mass communication practices. Indeed, media discourse is characterized by the simplification of issues, the reduction of complicated social, economic, or political matters to a rhetoric of pro and con, and the omission of ideologically inconsistent – or oppositional – narratives.

These developments are significant, because the images of the other that people carry in their heads depend almost exclusively on the flow of information that is provided by mass media and expedited by new technologies; this is true of domestic events, but it is particularly significant for events abroad, when direct knowledge fails altogether. The production of information – in the widest sense – has shifted from individual efforts, such as those of foreign correspondents, to wholesalers, such as news agencies, with severe consequences for the specificity or depth of information that comes with personal familiarity with a culture, including its language, and a sense of independence that is inherent in the work of journalists as intellectuals.

113

Instead, mass communication more typically – and in its traditional manifestations in newspapers, radio, or television – accommodates the processing of information that is predetermined by commercially or politically significant clients, predefined by public relations efforts, and preselected for specific uses in propaganda campaigns that range from advertising products to selling political ideas – such as war. It is a context of predictable ideological positioning of perspectives or arguments that makes for a one-dimensional view of the world, in which the prevailing idea is the dominant idea.

Since television remains the most popular source of identification of people and events, and because it is also the most affordable – and therefore by necessity the most desirable – medium, its impact on public knowledge is significant and its consequences are problematic. The initial "marketplace of ideas" notion of the media – which made mass communication philosophically an attractive, democratic option, because it could offer ideological alternatives and create alternative methods for scrutinizing information – has all but disappeared for a majority of the public, suggesting a realignment of the notion of audience in response to a decline in its involvement in making choices.

The reasons are twofold, with a focus on communicative and economic competencies. More specifically, the variety of ideas, world views, and opinions in the stream of mass communication – which is substantial and meaningful enough – remains inaccessible for larger segments of contemporary society, because they have neither the intellectual skills nor the economic means to take advantage of multiple resources. Consequently, definitions of the other, or reconstructions of the world, which could make a difference in the public's understanding of people or events, remain hidden, with the consequent failure to address the idea of participation as a public policy of educational and economic assistance for the disadvantaged – and therefore disenfranchised – members of society.

Moreover, such a failure undermines and destroys Habermas's idea of a "deliberative democracy," which embraces the ability to participate, equality of opportunity, and the autonomous formation of opinion in an ideal mass-communication environment, whose accessibility becomes a matter of political priorities. As a process of public meaning-making, mass communication contains the potential for competing constructions of reality with the presence of a variety of sources, including the internet. The social and political reality, however, is that dominant meanings are determined by the discursive practices of a handful of pervasive, and therefore politically powerful, media channels. Their representations of the world coincide frequently with dominant domestic and foreign policies and reflect (or reinforce) the contiguousness of commercial and political interests.

VI

The spatio-temporal framework that characterizes human existence is also reflected in the workings of mass communication, where it is a structural element not only of the process, but also of the discourse that yields the meanings of objects or events. It is characterized by the dimensions of "before and after" (between two events, for instance) and of "past–present–future" (as a historical perspective); both imply succession and change. The latter concept leads to the idea of motion and therefore to notions of time and space; it is embraced by communication – with the flow of words, the movement of the eyes across the page – and the practices of mass communication – with the linear design of books or the more complex visual narratives of film or television.

The process of mass communication is also a reminder of the time- and space-binding capacities of the media, and, more generally speaking, of the relationship between media and culture. Harold Innis considers the political organization of (ancient) empires, for instance, from the standpoint of time and space as inherent qualities of a variety of media and their contribution to the survival of a culture, and he suggests the importance of balance between space- and time-binding media in particular. Equally important, however, is the time-binding capacity of the individual, that is, the appropriation of past experiences, which includes the ability to condense history – and reality, in general – into a pattern of verbal or visual symbols with cultural implications for the appropriation, into the routines of daily existence, of space and time, which are codetermined by the process of mass communication.

The presence of mass communication in social relations, and its effects on the production of public knowledge also touch on constructions of time (or speed) and space; the latter are intuitions, according to Albert Einstein, that have become part of a social or cultural consciousness. The invention of photography, and of film as an extension of photography, is not only the historical moment marking the social awareness of a technology capable of reproducing the objective reality of the world – André Bazin calls film the art of reality – but also the start of a race to achieve instantaneousness by collapsing time, and to conquer space by reducing distance, with the aid of shutter speeds and long lenses respectively. The result is an enduring fiction that dominates subjective and objective perspectives on the world.

Mass communication forms an alliance with time and subjugates the narratives of knowledge to the dictates of speed. Ever since the shutter speed of the camera or the speed of the rotary press revealed new ways of capturing and preserving the moment, the technology of mass communication has continued to determine the pace of reproducing reality, with specific consequences for media content and effect. Thus, the leisurely pursuit of ideas in books or pamphlets has succumbed to the convenience of immediacy with the arrival of periodical literature – including newspapers with their new economy of space – only to capitulate finally to the possibilities of speed with the rise of electronic media.

In fact, time becomes arbitrary, from the pages of the novel to the film or television screen, when days can be compressed into a few sentences or seconds, while minutes can be stretched to last throughout an entire work, as in Joyce's *Ulysses*, which captures a day, or Godard's and Gorin's film *Letter to Jane*, which takes 45 minutes to analyze a single photograph of Jane Fonda in Hanoi. Likewise, the sequential nature of time, prevalent in printed narratives, is overcome by film or television, which may cut back and forth between concurrent actions and thus compile a more complex understanding of time, or relations between past and present. Even film techniques like slow or accelerated motion, or still photographs, are signifiers of the movement of time; their combination offers yet another experience of the arbitrariness of the moment.

116

Similarly, the perception of space may be significantly altered by film or television productions with the aid of lenses, combinations of shots, or even morphing. Types of shots are indicators of moods or conditions; for instance, Jean-Luc Godard once said that the close-up was invented for tragedy and the long shot for comedy, suggesting the range of technical choices for setting a scene. In fact, close-ups accentuate the (disembodied) face, without context but recognizable nevertheless. Close-ups are rarely achieved in real life, but an emphasis on the face reflects the cultural practices of contemporary mass communication. The media celebrate the face, which replaces the idea and serves to identify the individual with a cause while suggesting proximity, even intimacy, particularly in life-size representations on television screens.

In addition, montage fragments and reassembles reality to reconstitute time and space in narrative patterns, beyond the notion of merely editing a film sequence, and to provide an intellectual marker for contrast or conflict; an example is the originality of Sergei Eisenstein's work, which is grounded in the dialectical – the conflict of opposites. The disruption of the time continuum and the dissection of the spatial totality contain the substance for constructing meaning, which arises – in the readings of the spectator – from relationships among images that constitute the flow of the visual narrative.

But the notion of space beyond its physical or geographical def initions also includes the recognition of privacy as a constituent of social space. Mass communication typically crosses the boundaries of social space, technically through the process of dissemination and discursively through creative practices that invoke rights and insist on public interest. Indeed, mass communication, with its institutional regime of publicity, opposes the very notion of privacy by pursuing strategies of disclosure in the arena of information exchange, while elaborating on the conditions of privacy in fictional accounts with strategies of inclusion that obscure the difference between private and public and allow audiences to explore the intimacy of the other, including private thoughts.

When the need to protect privacy becomes an argument against the intrusion of mass communication, however, legal protection depends on the cultural or social specificity of the respective boundaries; the latter have been redrawn in the course of a history of increasing demands by the media for expansion into the territory of the private with arguments that their need to know – in the interest of public enlightenment – outweighs the individual's desire to be left alone. By and large the media have succeeded in overriding social or cultural concerns, not least because of the pressures of prurient interest, the promise of commercial gain, and the success of a journalism of exposure. Privacy, once a privilege of kings, has become a franchise of the mass media, which rule the definitions of its boundaries, while publicness, once the condition of democracy, has been reduced to an exercise of publicity.

But beyond strategic considerations of social space, issues of time, in particular, have gained new importance with the celebration of speed as a modern (or postmodern) contribution of technology to the field of mass communication. It manifests itself in the rise of computers with a new sense of time and speed. The result is a consuming, if not perverse, insistence on raising the quality of life by improving the power of operating systems by tenths of a second.

But the preoccupation with speed is much older and seems inherent in the development of communication technologies, beginning with faster printing presses and continuing with the speed of the telegraph and the electronic broadcasting delivery systems for making mass communication increasingly instantaneous – and therefore popular. Those technologies have also reoriented individuals towards notions of space and time by undermining patience and encouraging rupture or discontinuity, especially with the increasing speed of technological development itself during the last 20 years. Thus, there were 500 years between the invention of the printing press and the rise of photography, a few years between the employment of photography and the development of film and broadcasting, a couple of decades from this to the emergence of television, and only a generation until the arrival of satellite and computer technologies, whose expansion has become a continuous celebration of speed.

Indeed, speed dominates contemporary conceptualizations of mass communication as a determinant of its success, but it also dictates how individuals perceive the world. When it matters how fast news travels to its delivery points ("real news, real fast"), measured in minutes or seconds, broadcasting recasts the idea of experience in terms of subjective time. Consequently, listening, watching, or reading practices are informed by the time- and space-conscious nature of the process of mass communication; they affect understandings of duration or permanence and change. For instance, the 24-hour news cycles and the constant reminders of "breaking news" or "news alerts" by cable channels, the pace of news presentations, including the brevity and frequent intercutting of individual news items, the American montage of feature films or television series, together with contractions of geographical space with quick switches from coast to coast, or from continent to continent, are among the constitutive elements of a modern, accelerated spatio-temporal framework of social existence that is increasingly ahistorical and nomadic. Thus, people exist among the fragments of places and ideas that are offered reassuringly by mass communication as objective realities.

Speed upsets the balance between the space- and time-binding media, with considerable consequences for the survival of a culture. The privileging of space-binding – for instance with the aid of broadcasting media – serves mostly administrative purposes of social (and political) control through the production and dissemination of information. But when this occurs at the expense of the time-binding functions of print media, historical consciousness suffers, with the neglect of literature – and intellectual expression in general – whose contributions rely less on exploiting new technologies of mass communication and more on a contemplative mood and the art of reflection. A well-tempered process of mass communication in a democratic society not only reflects the balance between the immediacy of information-processing and the reach of historical knowledge, but must insist on the presence of both dimensions for the long-term benefits of a culture.

Nowadays the individual is confronted with a process of mass communication that incorporates and perpetuates a technological vision of communication; it builds on the speed of transfer and dissemination rather than on the need for understanding, and prefers the fragmentation of information to the integrity of explanation. Thus, newspapers carry shorter stories, newscasts contain items of shorter duration, and the complexity of social, economic, or political issues is reduced spatially and temporally to information bites, or visually to the imagery of disembodied faces.

The result is a short institutional attention span with a fading historical consciousness and a characteristic lack of concentration on issues or events beyond the realm of sensationalism. Such a vision excludes the possibility of maintaining a democratic perspective of inclusiveness and participation, particularly since the latter is based on negotiation and collaboration regarding time and space for the purposes of comprehending the issues of the day and scrutinizing the environment.

VII

The legacy of mass communication as a trustworthy producer and supplier of information, grounded in the history of the media and reinforced by self-promotion, is founded, among others, on claims of objectivity and neutrality that help drape journalism in a mantle of scientific respectability. It may be a methodological issue that insists on the passive or unbiased recording of objects or events, or a reference to the technical neutrality of the media machine, but it is also a larger cultural circumstance that encourages a belief in the unbiased nature of journalism, ever since the decline of a party press and the impact of commercial intent on the business of producing and disseminating information. Some time ago, the goal of supplying news and entertainment to the largest possible number of individuals encouraged American journalism, in particular, to develop a professional commitment to a discursive practice that is dedicated to objectivity and impartiality – at times redefined in terms of fairness to meet criticism – in the interest of serving a general public.

The emergence of the image as an increasingly relevant and legitimate element in the visual discourse has reinforced this commitment – based on the myth of the photograph, for instance, as an objective representation of reality – and strengthened the ideology of journalism as a documentary practice with deep roots in a belief in the availability of an impartial truth. After all, photographs are "the pencil of nature," as Fox Talbott assures us, and their uses in scientific and administrative work – ranging from medical research to criminal evidence – only reinforce the status of the image as the document of an objective truth.

The notion of objectivity in its journalistic application is also related to an ethics of mass communication, where it provides direction and closure for a professional practice which had been overshadowed in the past by acts of sensationalism, exaggeration, and fictionalization of information. Since objectivity is at the center of what journalism has meant, according to Michael Schudson, it has helped legitimize not only the profession, but also the industrial practices of media ownership. Indeed, objectivity is an institutional myth employed to maintain the status quo of media industries: internally to boost confidence in the power of professional integrity, and externally to confirm the dependability of the journalistic discourse and the credibility of the production of information.

Questions of objectivity ultimately raise expectations about truth claims that arise from the process of mass communication and burden journalistic practices; this is particularly so, when "news" and "truth" are used interchangeably, and "truth" is understood – in an elitist fashion – as an ultimate, authoritative answer that will dispel doubts and offer confidence in the power of journalism. Times of social, political, or economic uncertainty heighten the desire to know the truth and increase the responsibility of the media to confront public visions of news as truth with explanations about the existence of multiple truths, the centrality of discursive practices in articulating truths in specific historical moments, and the nature of constructing realities in general. After all, mass communication deals in approximations, because the quality of a discourse relies on the subjective knowledge and experience of those directing mass communication, which differs from the idealized knowledge and experience of a (democratic) public.

More generally, the trend towards an objectivist culture of mass communication, in which objects of knowledge have their own existence, obscures the identity of the source, and therefore the social or political context of the narrative; or, as Alvin Gouldner once observed, objectivism is a pathology of communication that remains silent about the speakers, their interests and desires, and how these interests are socially situated and structurally maintained. In

121

fact, anonymity – most rampant among visual representations on television produced by photographs and film or video clips – and lack of insight into the ideological make-up of those who construct reality and the social or political relation of knowledge to social formations, have contributed to the separation, if not isolation, of mass communication practices from public interest. There is no institutionally sanctioned participation – or partisanship, which is identified with specific voices (or faces) in the realm of mass communication – that allows for the biased or ideologically determined construction of knowledge as news, for instance.

Likewise, objectivity as a ritual of journalism reproduces an indefensible position regarding the disclosure of the interests and desires of journalists. In fact, it may even obstruct – or distort – the contributions of journalists, causing dissatisfaction among producers of information and an increasing level of misunderstanding among the public. Yet, recent developments leading to a concentration of news production, and to a reduction in the number of independent outlets, have reinforced if not strengthened the claims of news organizations regarding their integrity – that is, the objectivity of their constructions of reality. The reason may not be simple, but lack of access – combined with the ever-increasing complexity of social, political, and economic issues or policy decisions – has made it more difficult to establish counterclaims that expose the ideological nature of the news and the underlying political position of media organizations. In addition, it has become more complicated, if not impossible, for the public – in intellectual and economic terms – to switch to competing or alternative sources of information.

Consequently, exposure to the process of mass communication is not grounded in knowledge of – or in a partnership with – the public discourse, but in belief or trust in the representation of reality by a commercial institution whose dedication to the public interest is seriously undermined by the needs of a business culture. Such a trust is intuitive, it is typically based on past experience, ranging from the longevity of the relationship with media institutions and the availability of alternative sources of information or entertainment, to degrees of satisfaction with the style and content of the media discourse. At times audiences are in a position to judge standards of accuracy (the chronicling of local events, for instance);

in other instances, standards of trust are based on ideological grounds, even on pure empathy with particular topics, or on a personal attraction to a style of presentation – and a presenter – rather than on the quality of the content.

In any case, there is no effective recourse, legal or otherwise, for an audience in the event of incomplete or faulty information – besides libel, slander, or invasion of privacy. There may be an appeal to honesty or the maintenance of standards, but the process of mass communication lacks guarantees that protect against untruthfulness or error and operates on retaining audience confidence. There is also an assumption that personal judgment, based on competence or satisfaction, must guide the ultimate decision regarding trust in the objectivity of the public discourse. But given the pervasiveness of mass communication in all of its forms and its total penetration of the public sphere, the cancellation of a newspaper, or a cable television service, the refusal to watch television or listen to radio, even the rejection of literature as a source of insights, may not resolve problems of mistrust. Public knowledge and experience continue to rely on the flow of mass-mediated realities that are reflected in the daily conversations that permeate the public sphere. There is no escape from the collective world view of a media industry that seems less divided over the discursive strategies of representation, including the ideological thrust of the discourse, than over territorial issues pertaining to influence and control over the public sphere.

There is a new objectivity, however, expressed in an active language that challenges the traditional myth of (American) journalism, with a disclosure of identity and ideology and an insistence on fairness and accuracy that gives a new meaning to the relationship between mass communication and public interest. It is a practice that is most typically – but not exclusively – identified with marginal media, which oppose and confront the hegemonies of knowledge production that define social, economic, and political realities – and which strive to offer alternative world views that are based on knowledge as a cultural construction at a concrete historical moment. By taking this approach they hope to secure public participation in a critique of traditional constructions of reality that encourages independent thought regarding the shape of the world.

After all, mass communication does contain the potential for redefining the notion of objectivity to become culturally determined, discursively defined, and inclusive of multiple, even contradictory, ideological positions. The recovery of the social or political potential of society includes the legitimation of creative possibilities in a collaborative atmosphere of constructing working realities that are conscious of the media reality.

VIII

The network of mass communication that surrounds and interacts with society like a web of signs and symbols is best described by references to "flow" and "intertextuality," which suggest the filmic, self-referential quality of an individual's experience of media exposure.

The idea of "flow" is used in this context to describe the actual movement of signs, or items, along a temporal or spatial dimension involving all means of mass communication, from print to broadcast media, and embracing notions of programming or layout. This understanding of media content (information and entertainment) as "flow" also includes commercial messages – that is, the classified advertisement or the broadcast commercial – in a grand narrative that weaves fact and fiction into the reality of everyday life. Distinctions of genres or categories of conventions, from melodrama to op-ed material, disappear. They are replaced by selected impressions of media activities that cut across a traditional, media-induced compartmentalization of contents and constitute the cultural resource for the real-life practices of people; they also inform the social, political, or economic knowledge, opinions, and attitudes of people. The flow of mass communication in its size and diversity, however, also reflects the vigor and quality of a culture, its profoundness or simplicity, as well as its preoccupations with issues and events. It is an advertisement of its strengths and weaknesses, but also an open invitation to share its offerings through a process of immersion in series of sequences that feature multiple encounters with versions of reality in a permanent flow of verbal and visual cues.

Thus, material objects, people, or events and immaterial feelings or ideas are produced, defined, described, and sometimes reproduced for emphasis; feelings or ideas are reconstructed in language or visual performances with growing confidence in the workings of the public imagination, for instance when it comes to understanding and constructing the meaning of film narratives, literary genres, or journalistic styles. Individuals encounter the narratives of mass communication as a matter of course; they are involved in the daily routines of making sense of a world of events and opinions that exists solely in media reproductions and is disclosed through drawing on a familiarity with culture and society that comes from memory and history.

In fact, the notion of "flow" suggests a proximity to film or to the experience with surfaces and interiors that unites literature and film and extends beyond them to other media. Exposure to the narratives of the media, in general, is a social event that involves individuals whose collective consciousness is reconstituted in notions of spectatorship, audience, or readership. Like film, which needs to specify its audience, the media must also engage in efforts – beyond advertising – to attract and keep individuals through developing a type of brand recognition or genre loyalty. The latter is frequently established with the aid of personalities, or movie stars, whose presence is apt to guarantee popularity and success of the medium. The construction of stars or personalities occurs through the combined efforts of different media, from fanzines to the daily press, and from broadcasting to film and television, and helps chart a specific course of consumption for the individual fan. The latter is interested not only in the activities of favorite personalities, but uses them – like the imagery of people in general – to materialize issues or ideas, such as social or political positions or more abstract philosophical notions.

The "flow" of mass communication offers representations that serve specific purposes for specific audiences, although not everybody participates in this process, since rising prices – and increasing sophistication – make attending to the "flow" of mass communication an elitist practice. For instance, while movie-going accentuates growing social and cultural differences, television watching supports the idea of universal availability in a society which is characterized by decreasing media accessibility for the working class and increasing reinforcement of a bourgeois media culture.

Nevertheless, attending to the "flow" is a notable moment in an individual's search for identity, because it occurs at the site of desire, once described by Sigmund Freud as the gap between the real and the imaginary. The media are located in this gap. They require people to see or listen, and looking (as well as hearing) will stimulate the imagination. Thus, meaning-making refers to the gaze of an audience and its longings for the objects of desire, which may include conditions of existence or a state of mind, through culturally and socially determined narratives. Under these circumstances, the "flow" of mass communication becomes a voyeuristic experience in which people identify with the process, that is, with the eye of the camera or with the perspective of the journalist/writer. By collapsing the differences between individuals and the respective media apparatus, reality is no longer a media representation, but an instance of personal perception; in fact, the media not only constitute people's social, cultural, and political context, but they also merge with individual identity. Individuals embrace the subject position of their idols in dress, speech, and behavior: as readers, they are a part of the text.

Unable, however, to also possess — or completely internalize and control — the media reality, individuals continue to be fascinated by particular forms of representation; searching for the perfect match, they are drawn to watch, read, or listen to their favorite sequences in the "flow" of mass communication. Yet unlike film, which offers a complete narrative — from beginning to end — the "flow" of mass communication continues to produce sequences over time from a variety of media, which reinforces a permanent state of becoming. Since an understanding about being in the world always remains a partial experience, the process of mass communication invites individuals to complete this experience by creating their own paths through representations of existence with the help of selective retention, reflection or consciousness, and preferred readings, although the outcome of these applications is most likely determined by social formations such as class, gender, or ethnicity.

126

It is the process of the montage, however – a selection of representations of objects or events, claimed from media presentations and reorganized in a rapid succession of sequences – that reconstitutes a single view of a vague reality, or a coherent and ideologically consistent statement about people or events. For André Bazin, speaking about film, montage is essentially and by its nature opposed to the expression of ambiguity. Thus, montage is the reflection of an attitude of certainty that comes with the intent and purpose of the producer. In the context of exploring the process of mass communication in general, montage is an intervention, or a process of editing the "flow" of mass communication, that exists as an individual response to social or cultural demands for making sense of the world. Perfected by images or words from across a variety of media, the montage expresses a particular *Weltanschauung* of the individual as monteur, whose needs for reinforcement or confirmation are met by securing only what is relevant or important from the "flow" of mass communication. The idea of montage, then, suggests the employment of choice in a departure from a holistic view of the process of mass communication, a devotion to parts or sequences of the "flow" for a specific, ideologically predisposed reading.

The effort of positioning the individual within the complex articulations of reality, however, is complicated by the degree of knowledge regarding the popular narratives of the cultural discourse. It is also influenced by the increasingly close relationship between texts, together with an increasing willingness to rely on self-referential strategies within a specific medium, such as the novel, but also across media, as for example between television drama and newspaper reports. This intertextuality of the subject marks contemporary popular culture production and suggests not only a wide and varied cultural consumption, but cultural literacy sufficient for a sophisticated reading of the respective texts.

Underlying these approaches to the process of mass communication is a respect for reality, its representation in media narratives, and its reproduction by the individual for the purpose of understanding life. Although most closely related to the capabilities of photography and film to freeze the moment and capture the natural world, the revelation of reality is a concern throughout media practices – and a major social or cultural function. In fact, a revelation of that which is "real" is the outstanding attraction of media fare.

IX

The process of mass communication is also a process of authentication, which orders or categorizes, describes, and displays a day's events – or the course of a life – in a wide variety of verbal and visual narratives. As such, mass communication serves the construction of a dominant version of history that is based on the ruling ideas in society. In fact, the media are typically recorders of past events: they chronicle experiences, and they produce sets of circumstances that are merged in the making of an instant historical record. The rush to history is inherent in the process of mass communication, which is increasingly defined by notions of speed. Thus, where historians customarily reject premature constructions of history, the media are busily engaged in the fabrication of historical narratives; the latter attempt to make sense of complex and immediate social or political developments, either in a competitive spirit or in an effort to ensure social stability.

Indeed, the media – and the presence of television in particular – offer a sense of social or political stability through a constant flow of information; it is the fact of being there reliably that is otherwise sought in family values or religious practices. The latter also provide a historical dimension (in the form of customs or traditions), which is recreated by mass communication with its self-referential presence in subjective, dynamic, and relational narratives about the world, which help determine the form and content of historical consciousness. Furthermore, this process is often encased in commercial sponsorship – not unlike the way in which advertising embraces media narratives – when institutions of mass communication, such as museums (the Smithsonian, for instance), rely on corporate support to define the essence of American social or cultural history.

Social or political history is always biographical in the sense of having touched the lifeworld of individuals; it becomes self-serving class biography, however, when the narrative turns into a mass-mediated discourse mainly of those preoccupied with securing their own place in history. Privileged historical narratives cater to bourgeois demands for conservation of the bourgeois image in the realm of mass communication. By controlling media (and media content), the dominant class fixes its own historical position and reinforces the presence of the corporate world in the public sphere. In other words, mass communication serves the interests of a specific class, whose image survives in media practices, while those whose interests are missing from the societal dialogue – and the content of the media – are also marginalized in the historical record.

For instance, it has taken much longer for biographies of the economically and politically exploited to emerge – as in the work of Howard Zinn, for instance, and other social historians since the 1960s. A public narrative of history, like the Vietnam war memorial in Washington, DC, remains a celebrated exception to the rule of corporate sponsorship. The fate of ordinary people is more often represented – and immortalized – in fictional accounts, including songs and poetry. Indeed, fiction, and the aesthetic dimension in general, constitutes an alternative source of historical insight that has rarely been used for understanding society's own definitions and uses of mass communication. Yet cultural practice, including the arts, contributes steadily to the discourse of society by redefining and reproducing the tendencies of the time, including the reconceptualization of the media and the process of mass communication.

More often than not, however, history is constructed in an established, top-down fashion with an ideologically informed depiction of a past that has been authenticated and preserved in the process of mass communication. The resulting one-dimensional narrative typically features institutional power and celebrates charismatic leadership while misrepresenting or neglecting the material or ideational contributions of ordinary people as citizens, neighbors, or colleagues. However, when the oppressed or forgotten realize the power of their own historical narrative and its inherent threat to the status quo, their interest in history – to use the words of Günter Anders – may well confirm an appetite for rebellion.

The idea of mass communication as history, on the other hand, suggests a more aggressive use of media power in the construction of a reality that foreshadows the future. The ease, for instance, with which journalism changes into history as news accounts are turned into book-length treatments of specific topics, such as Columbine, Afghanistan, or 9/11, is a useful example of the merger of mass communication and history as storytelling. But the practice is also suggestive of a commercially driven anticipation of historically significant events as lucrative opportunities for shaping public discourse. It explains the impatience of the producer, who embraces the trend toward journalism as history, which is based on speed, legitimated by its own success in the public sphere, and confirmed by its own replication over time and across media.

Moreover, mass communication as history suggests the complete collapse of the past into the present – a denial of history in its traditional role – and its replacement by speculation without historical consciousness. Mass communication destroys history, replacing it with journalism as an explanatory apparatus that meets a public need for instantaneous interpretation. The latter is based on the myth of fairness and objectivity in the process of mass communication to explicate matters and assign meanings in a detached and unbiased manner.

History is by and large a public narrative that is rarely used (by journalism) as a method of explaining contemporary conditions. The lack of historical consciousness is evident in news coverage, in particular, which is void of historical insight and represents people or events in a self-contained, ahistorical, and fragmented manner. Yet history is also a critical method of inquiry which reveals the ideologically charged conduct of mass communication and the processes of manipulation or mystification that have marked media performances. Such a process of demystification rests on the strength of memory and the ability of individuals to recall the promises of media routines in a democratic society. In fact, remembering past performances and scrutinizing the present positions of the means of mass communication help recast the role of the media and address their social responsibility. Thus, questions of mass communication and history may also be posed as questions about the power of memory. Grounded in language, memory is also an essential element of individual or collective identity in the course of shaping the history of a culture.

The idea of mass communication and history rests in the capacity to capture memory – as in the photograph, the video recording, or the novel – when memory turns into material history and remains embedded in individual or collective thought; there it grounds experience and the time and place of existence and infuses a vocabulary that speaks to issues of identity and being in the world. Memory also constitutes the power of bringing the lessons of history to bear on the issues of mass communication which may confront those seeking to create a different kind of democratic system of communication. For this reason it is important to engage in the act of remembering purposefully, with an awareness of past tendencies, especially when – as Leo Lowenthal observes – what is remembered and what is forgotten are almost indistinguishable, and purely the result of chance.

X

The coverage of the terrorist assault on Manhattan and Washington reveals the limits of mass communication. Those limits reside in the substance as well as in the practices of mass communication, beginning with the problems of television production, specifically, and ending with the blurred boundaries of perception between a mediated reality and the reality of the disaster.

Shortly after the moment of the attack and time and again after the initial shock, people at the scene kept saying that the television images in their living rooms were nothing compared to the reality on the ground. They were stunned as much by the realization that the media had been unable to convey the reality of the events as by the extent of the human catastrophe itself. Their presence at the scene of the disaster revealed the poverty of mass communication. Reduced to a mere marker of a historical event, television was blinded by its inherent inability to absorb and reproduce its totality, physically and emotionally, reducing the attempt to convey the horror of the moment to the repetitive presentation of spectacular images.

As a strategy of maintaining interest and drawing viewers into the program, repetition quickly becomes an annoyance and, more importantly, reduces the construction of the event to a television happening by relying on the standard language of television production. In addition, the horrific imagery becomes just too good not to be used over and over again in a cycle of violence that numbs rather than enlightens the viewer. Thus, while taking advantage of what television does best – being at the scene – coverage of 9/11 also overreached its potential when it wanted to be what it could not be: a pair of searching eyes of a thinking and feeling individual on the ground at a catastrophic event. The incident also revealed that television pictures are not worth a thousand words, and suggested that journalistic products remain fragmented performance pieces which leave no time for reflection about a television reality which is but a simulation of being at the scene.

Because looking involves the human capacity for emotion, the experience of being in a place or with people makes the encounter with "news" a different adventure. Thus, there were many references to the cinematic quality of the unfolding tragedy. Comments from viewers – "it was like in the movies" or "this was like television" – only confirmed that individuals live with and react to the defining authority of mass communication and its impact on how they experience the world. Consequently, if it is television, it may be easier to bear, since it is not real, but if it is real, it is still television.

Since mass communication operates within a technological and ideological frame, fragmentation rules the process of mediation; that is, reality is always produced within the size of a television screen, a newspaper column, or a broadcast minute as well as within the boundaries of professional standards and political ambitions. The raw and unedited personal experience of 9/11, however, stayed outside these customary media frames, overlapping perhaps in its sequencing of events; but it was larger, more comprehensive, felt more deeply, and, above all, it was visceral. Being there was a deeply personal experience, in which the camera was replaced by looking, which called upon all of the senses for an emotional response; it was also a shared experience among strangers, when passive media audiences, released into their own reality, turned into responsive and caring individuals.

When people became aware of the limitations of mass communication, it was a realization that turned into a moment of liberation from the confining aspects of "live" coverage and the narrow physical and ideological frame that mass communication provided during those first hours after the attack. At that time, communication among individuals reasserted itself as an appropriate and comforting practice that drew people together, made sharing their grief more tolerable, and corrected – at least for a while – the imbalance between communication and mass communication that characterizes contemporary existence. With it came a turn from the restrictive notion of the act as a preferred form of participation in the world of media, for instance (which must be bought, or switched on, and followed) to the idea of activity (which signals involvement in the process of constructing subjective realities) as a liberating practice among individuals.

Since then, mass communication has been used to exploit the emotional vulnerability of society and has re-established itself as the defining context for constructing victimhood, assigning blame, and supporting retaliation to cultivate an unsettled social climate in which to sell a host of ideologically determined political responses to questions of guilt, and to promote military solutions.

XI

The problem of mass communication is its domination as a supplier of knowledge and its pervasiveness as a producer of social and political realities; regardless of whether one participates in the process as viewer, reader, or listener, it becomes impossible to escape from the effects of a mediated social existence. For many individuals, mass communication has succeeded in transforming the world into pictures, and their lives into a reflection on a television screen. The confrontation with mass communication is a lifelong experience. It shapes not only the discourse of society, but also the minds of individuals, who struggle with making meaning – based on knowledge supplied by the media in order to make sense of their complex, mediated environment – or who submit without regret to the agenda-setting initiatives of mass communication.

Moreover, the social and political problem of mass communication is also a problem of relationships between the individual and the institution and over issues of participation. Since the question is not about manipulation, but about who manipulates, the owner-ship of the means of mass communication becomes a major concern, as does the social responsibility of such ownership vis-à-vis the ability to communicate, which includes the acquisition of communicative competence and access to the media forum. The latter remains an unsettled yet central issue for the success of a democratic system of communication.

The issue of participation is embedded in the idea of sharing, which is an ethical dimension of social communication, particularly in a capitalist society, in which the distribution of wealth and the control of essential industries based on finite resources, including the media, pose major problems related to equality, fairness, and equal opportunity. Sharing remains an appealing idea; indeed, democracy holds a deep attraction for sharing not only material but also spiritual goods.

Many years ago, Charles Sanders Peirce advocated the use of love against the advances of greed as he stood up against the symbols of capitalism in America. Today we know that communities of love have failed to make a difference, but radical thought still carries the seed of change. Such thought must find its way into mainstream media to contribute to the construction of alternatives in politics, economics, and society in general. It includes the process of mass communication, which remains connected to the major policy arenas of society, where it shapes the language – and therefore life as we know it.

But the right to a democratic form of life – as a constitutional guarantee – is also the right to communicate, and the right to com-municate in the twenty-first century must include the use of dia-logue and the right of access to the means of mass communication. While the former is a characteristic of human relationships, the latter is an economic issue of affordability and a legal issue of secur-ing space and time from the media for the purposes of public par-ticipation. Yet participation may be difficult to achieve, because mass communication represents the power of the monologue, sometimes disguised as dialogue, but in the end always a one-sided engagement with objects or ideas that makes for an unevenness between insti-tutional claims on the sphere of communication and individual needs for expression beyond the anticipated response to media practices.

When Robert Hutchins concludes that the civilization of the dialogue is the only civilization worth having and the only one in which the whole world can unite, he suggests a strategy of communication which is human and acknowledges the unending significance of individuality. His approach also relegates mass communication to a subordinate position in the realm of human practices. Dialogue is mutual and requires persistence in communication, which is crucial for understanding the self and respecting differences while finding common ground. And when Mikhail Bakhtin proclaims that to be means to communicate dialogically, he moves the spirit of communication to the center of social existence. Thus, it is the process of communicating with others that needs to be addressed, particularly in efforts to help overcome the modern experience of separateness, which is a source of anxiety, misunderstanding, and ultimately of defeat.

Dialogue also assumes the presence of differences, but the process of mass communication typically encourages conformity, particularly in its information function, eliminates differences of taste or opinion, often in the name of equality or democracy, and reinforces institutional desires for social control. On the other hand, mass communication, in the form of creative and philosophical practices, is at its best, when it inspires dialogical relationships that retain and strengthen individual identities and reject conformity as a sign of equality. Dialogue becomes an expression of sociability and, therefore, helps restore the power of communication in the struggle for survival in a conformist society; it also is a reminder of the importance of what George Herbert Mead has called the generalized other in the development of the self.

The process of mass communication teaches, above all, that individuation is easily reduced to a working commercial or political ideology rather than acknowledged as a presupposition for an emerging dialogical existence. Indeed, dialogue is in decline as the other has been replaced by the process of mass communication, which rearticulates the idea of dialogue in terms of production and consumption and annihilates the state of authentic being. Differently expressed, mass communication relies on an ideological sanction of individual autonomy in the process of exploiting individuality to serve mass culture, according to Leo Lowenthal.

Dialogue is not merely compliance or agreement, but also a confrontation of differences and an expansion of knowledge. Mass communication in its traditional form of press or broadcasting, on the other hand, rarely challenges the intellectual limits of its audiences, but promotes ease and efficiency of comprehension. If language is a dimension of life – or, following Ludwig Wittgenstein, if the limits of language are the limits of the world – then life seems to be a simple and straightforward matter, according to the performances of mass communication. There is no desire on the part of the media to improve words or images, or to teach – and therefore introduce the complexities of life – by reconceptualizing the media as educational institutions in society. On the contrary, Neil Stephenson's caustic comment in *Snow Crash* that eventually Americans will excel in only four practices, music, film, software, and fast home delivery of pizza, also seems to foreshadow a shift in mass communication that is characterized by a loss of dialogue and an absence of ordinary language. This neglect, given the low quality of formal education, may have disastrous consequences for the future of a society in which an undereducated population is not only unable to articulate its concerns, but is also highly susceptible to mass persuasion – and therefore to control.

Since mass communication continues to accommodate special interests, which prevail with the spread of more nonessential, fragmented, and simplified information rather than with relevant explanations for their respective audiences, the task of clarification has fallen to civic groups, frequently operating outside the commitment of a media industry to business and politics. Yet, it remains difficult for individual or collective ideas to reach the public sphere when that sphere is described as a market and controlled by media organizations. The latter engage in defining the parameters of information – as well as the world of fiction – with absolute certainty and render the circulation of their factual or fictional materials effective.

The news item or the novel, the film or the song, are the work of intellectual or creative activities that are coopted and commodified to become subject to ideologically sensitive, commercial specifications. There is a market even for oppositional ideas, which are ultimately embraced by the dominant forces in the realm of media practices. This process shapes the boundaries of the social and cultural realities that determine individuals and their outlook on the world.

Mass communication, in other words, creates the conditions – and provides the knowledge – under which people live, judge their environment, and make choices that determine their future. The experts of Lippmann's complex world, who were to be the guides through the maze of facts and figures, finding truth and avoiding falsehood, are now in charge. But instead of working for the public good they serve those in control of the means of mass communication, who ask the questions and determine the agenda.

Mass communication has accompanied the rise of Western civilization with increasing technological sophistication that has kept pace with the scientific advances of society. Those advances have led to the domination of a technological rationale that has engaged the means of mass communication to secure the functioning of the societal apparatus. Thus, ideas of community, democracy, or freedom have been employed in the service of an ideology that grounds mass communication in the dominant politico-economic order. Indeed, after centuries of exposure to the ideas of democracy (and individual liberty), it still seems that the beliefs and institutions of democracy have never become fully separated from commercial interests, from where they developed, as Reinhold Niebuhr suggested in the 1930s. Mass communication legitimates their power and operationalizes claims of social integration with confidence in a flow of mass communication that shapes the "objective" reality which determines the discourse of society.

Such a flow, however, is determined by a lack of choice, and by excess, and imbalance, which characterize the historical development of mass communication. The challenge of a cultural policy of choice, liberated from the adverse social and economic conditions affecting too many people, remains a limited individual option. For instance, instead of reinforcing the idea of reading – a flourishing practice of past civilizations – which confirms the status of the book, and the arts in general, as sources of knowledge, there is excessive exposure to television, or a celebration of the phatic image, as sources of distraction. The result is a cultural imbalance that caters to commercial demands and social control rather than to individual needs and private encounters with ideas. Gustave Flaubert's suggestion, read in order to live, seems quite appropriate in the context of searching for a balance between the authenticity of the self in communication (and in the process of learning) and the collective dependence on mass communication (and the manner of experience).

Thus, the notion of mass communication as a technologically driven, partisan social agent is reinforced by its historical progression – from the rise of the printing press, which strengthened bourgeois control, to the breakthrough of television, which confirmed the power of corporate capitalism. Subsequently, mass communication has been further politicized by privileging the information needs of a shrinking middle or upper class that relies on print media, while others live with the inevitability of broadcast entertainment. These differences have become more pronounced as time passes. In fact, the aristocratic patronage system of the Middle Ages, which supported creative and intellectual work that was accessible only to bourgeois elites, has been successfully extended in modernity by corporate sponsorship of narratives that shape the contemporary reality of the masses.

In the meantime, mass communication creates an atmosphere of enforced tolerance that contributes to the success of the political system, the changing nature of democracy, and to the ways in which individuals acquire their identities. For instance, between the lack of campaign financing reforms – which must satisfy the wealthy classes – and recent infringement of civil rights – which must please the dominant bureaucratic class – the interests and rights of US citizens have been marginalized with the aid of the popular media and television journalism, in particular, which have recreated the individual as subject. These media benefit financially from political advertising and have long ignored, if not forgotten, the original calling of the fourth estate as a watchdog for all of the people. Now more than ever, the presence of an independent and critical press (or media system in general) is crucial not only for the function of democracy at a time of national and international crises, but also for the reinforcement of democratic practices among individuals and their exchange of ideas in the context of national or regional debates in the public sphere.

Mass communication offers a historically grounded discourse of self in society that reflects an uneven distribution of power as it continues to move further away from serving a public with the informed prejudice and the knowledgeable interest that characterize an authentic commitment to the cause of liberty.

XII

Mass communication in the twenty-first century is the context of being in the world, it originates the destabilized milieu of fact and fiction that creates the media reality in which individuals live and die. As such, the historical process of mass communication has broken down traditional boundaries, like those between journalism and literature, to operate in an atmosphere of multiple knowledges and truths. The result is a new cultural form, which is characterized not only by intertextuality and inter-mediality, pervasiveness and speed, but also by an assimilation of its audience. With a collapse of the boundaries between production and consumption – or between spectacle and spectator, when the image becomes the real, and the real merges with the image – audiences may begin to understand that they reside within the text of their media reality. They will recognize themselves in the mirror-image of the media, as they are the mirror-image of media representations in their gestures, speech, and ideologies. Media reality is the assimilation of the lifeworld through the process of mass communication and a cultural context for acting upon the demands of the here and now – which is the dominant reality.

Mass communication is the postmodern version of a cultural life that consists of a montage of meanings and knowledges of individuals, who try to make sense of their own existence. They do so by drawing on the experience of living in a media reality, which informs the manner of their interpretation and confirms their claim to knowledge. The search for "the" truth – although never fully abandoned – has turned into settling for multiple possibilities, which destabilize the boundaries between continuity and discontinuity of social, political, or economic conditions. Yet the media go on creating myths that are compatible with the desire for stability, including the permanence of the political or economic control of the dominant class.

Under these circumstances the gaze of the critical observer must shift to the destabilized relations between communication and mass communication, whose boundaries collapsed some time ago with the rise of modern media, when the conditions of community were replaced by the practice of consumerism, or when the milieu of mass communication embraced the lifeworld of the individual. Most recently, this milieu has extended into a virtual reality, where the autonomy of communication through dialogue is further undermined by the desire for soliloquies in the confines of a virtual space.

A lack of authentic communication is the result of the art of chatter, to use Martin Heidegger's phrase, which is represented by mass communication and reflects the deterioration of *Dasein* as a condition of being with others. Indeed, existence is defined by an ability to remain in communication not only with others, but also with oneself as a source of genuine feeling for one's environment. The blurring of distinctions between communication and mass communication not only redefines and confirms the role of media as the other, but reduces the self to a representation of an anonymous and alienated existence in the grasp of mass communication. Thus, the struggle over regaining access to communication is a struggle for selfhood and for relations with others, freed from both the isolation of the self and the embrace of organized mass communication.

Furthermore, media reality as a preeminent and dynamic social milieu raises questions about its relations to other (political and economic) forms of domination – including relations between commercial intent and political will and authorship and control of its ideological substance – and reinforces inquiries about the political economy of the means of mass communication. This is especially true under the changing circumstances of a postmodern existence, in which temporary contracts are supplanting permanent institutions in the realm of professional, cultural, political, and international affairs, according to Jean-François Lyotard.

Consequently one must ask, what are the expectations for mass communication to advance democratization and for how long? What is the investment of economic capital in support of a politics of equality and justice through cultural practices in a rapidly changing world and in an ideological environment with crumbling borders? That is, what must be done, when the lines between democratic capitalism and fascism are obscured, and their goals become indistinguishable, when mass communication aestheticizes politics by creating myths of community and nation, and of harmony and the stability of social values?

The dominant discourse of mass communication furnishes the cultural capital for negotiating the construction of reality among individuals or between individuals and institutions. These (rhetorical) acts of individual or collective agency occur within the boundaries of mass communication, however, from where new instruments of domination – in the form of persuasion and suppression – emerge, to replace traditional (political or social) authorities of legitimation. As a result, words and images instead of police control society, popular media instead of prisons confine individuals, and media practices instead of personal communication determine the nature of self and others; that is, hitherto fixed institutions of authority are effectively replaced by movable (or easily adaptable) instruments of control.

The idea of mass communication has come a long way in the company of power relations surrounded by an enduring pursuit of knowledge and hopes of liberation. Still, as a constituent element of the historical process of public communication, including various forms of public persuasion – such as propaganda, advertising, public relations, and journalism – mass communication continues to represent the economic and political authority of the dominant order, from where it creates the realities of self and society and dispenses its myths for the masses as prescribed by the routines of the spectacle.

Bibliography

Where appropriate, the original date of publication is indicated first.

1 Mass Communication and the Promise of Democracy

Adams, Samuel Hopkins. 1909. In *Colliers* 43 (22 May).

Althusser, Louis. 1971. *Lenin and Philosophy and Other Essays.* London: New Left Books.

Aquinas, Thomas. 1256–70/1952. In Petrus Hoennen. *Reality and Judgment according to St. Thomas.* Chicago: Regnery.

Arendt, Hannah. 1958. *The Human Condition: A Study of the Central Dilemmas Facing Modern Man.* Chicago: University of Chicago Press.

Augustine. 397–8/1961. *Confessions.* Baltimore: Penguin Books.

Bagdikian, Ben H. 1983/1997. *The Media Monopoly.* Boston: Beacon Press.

Barthes, Roland. 1957/1972. *Mythologies.* London: Jonathan Cape.

Barzan, Paul A., and Paul M. Sweeney. 1966. *Monopoly Capital: An Essay on the American Economic and Social Order.* New York: Monthly Review Press.

Baudrillard, Jean. 1981. *For a Critique of the Political Economy of the Sign.* St. Louis, MO: Telos Press.

Baudrillard, Jean. 1988. *America.* London: Verso.

Becker, Howard Paul. 1956. *Modern Sociological Theory in Continuity and Change.* New York: Dryden Press.

Bell, Daniel. 1976. *The Cultural Contradictions of Capitalism.* New York: Basic Books.

Bibliography

Benjamin, Walter. 1986. *Reflections: Essays, Aphorisms, Autobiographical Writings*, ed. Peter Demetz. New York: Schocken Books.

Bernays, Edward. 1923. *Crystallizing Public Opinion*. New York: Boni and Liveright.

Blumer, Herbert. 1939. In Robert E. Park, ed. *An Outline of the Principles of Sociology*. New York: Barnes & Noble.

Braudel, Fernand. 1973. *Capitalism and Material Life, 1400–1800*. New York: Harper & Row.

Bryce, James. 1889. *The American Commonwealth*. Indianapolis: Liberty Fund.

Camus, Albert. 1979. *The Essential Writings*, ed. Robert E. Meagher. New York: Harper & Row.

Cassirer, Ernst. 1944. *An Essay on Man*. New Haven: Yale University Press.

Cicero, Marcus Tullius. 55 B.C./1967. *De Oratore*, ed. E. W. Sutton and H. Rackham. Cambridge, MA: Harvard University Press.

Commission on Freedom of the Press. 1947. *A Free and Responsible Press. A General Report on Mass Communication: Newspapers, Radio, Motion Pictures, Magazines and Books*. Chicago: University of Chicago Press.

Comte, Auguste. 1853/1975. *Auguste Comte and Positivism*, ed. Gertrud Lenzer. The Essential Writings. New York: Harper & Row.

Corey, Lewis. 1935. *The Crisis of the Middle Class*. New York: Covici Friede.

Creel, George. 1947. *Rebel at Large*. New York: Putnam.

Dahrendorf, Ralph. 1970. In Philip Rief, ed. *On Intellectuals: Theoretical Studies, Case Studies*. New York: Anchor Books.

Debord, Guy. 1992. *Society of the Spectacle and other Films*. London: Rebel Press.

Dewey, John. 1916. *Democracy and Education: An Introduction to the Philosophy of Education*. New York: Macmillan.

Dewey, John. 1927. *The Public and its Problems*. New York: Henry Holt.

Downie, Leonard Jr., and Robert G. Kaiser. 2002. *The News about the News*. New York: Knopf.

Durkheim, Emile. 1893/1947. *The Division of Labor in Society*. Glencoe, IL: Free Press.

Enzensberger, Hans-Magnus. 1974. *The Consciousness Industry: On Literature, Politics and the Media*. New York: Seabury Press.

Foucault, Michel. 1972/1980. *Power/Knowledge: Selected Interviews and Other Writings, 1972–1977*. New York: Pantheon Books.

Gerbner, George. 1967. In Frank E. X. Dance, ed. *Human Communication Theory: Original Essays*. New York: Holt, Rinehart & Winston.

Goethe, Johann Wolfgang von. 1795/1901. *Wilhelm Meister's Apprenticeship*. Boston: Nicolls.

Gramsci, Antonio. 1948–51/1971. *Selections from the Prison Notebooks*, ed. Quintin Hoare and Geoffrey Nowell Smith. New York: International Publishers.

Habermas, Jürgen. 1962/1989. *The Structural Transformation of the Public Sphere: An Inquiry into a Category of Bourgeois Society.* Cambridge, MA: MIT Press.

Hall, Stuart. 1979. In James Curran, Michael Gurevitch, and Janet Woollacott, eds. *Mass Communication and Society.* Beverly Hills, CA: Sage.

Hardt, Michael, and Antonio Negri. 2000. *Empire.* Cambridge, MA: Harvard University Press.

Herman, Edward S., and Noam Chomsky. 1988. *Manufacturing Consent: The Political Economy of the Mass Media.* New York: Pantheon.

Horkheimer, Max. 1941. Notes on Institute Activities. *Zeitschrift für Sozialforschung*, 9:1, 121–3.

Horkheimer, Max, and Theodor W. Adorno. 1944/1972. *Dialectic of Enlightenment.* New York: Herder & Herder.

Hovland, Carl I. 1949. In Carl I. Hovland, Arthur A. Lumsdaine, and Fred D. Sheffield. *Experiments on Mass Communication.* Princeton: Princeton University Press.

Innis, Harold. 1950/1972. *Empire and Communication.* Toronto: University of Toronto Press.

Jefferson, Thomas. 1944. *Writings of Thomas Jefferson*, vol. 4, ed. Philip S. Foner. New York: Wiley Books.

Jouhaud, Christian. 1987. In Roger Chartier, ed. *The Culture of Print. Power and the Uses of Print in Early Modern Europe.* Princeton: Princeton University Press.

Kant, Immanuel. 1781/1952. *The Critique of Pure Reason.* Chicago: Encyclopedia Britannica.

Kant, Immanuel. 1788/1998. *The Critique of Practical Reason.* Milwaukee: Marquette University Press.

Keane, John. 1991. *The Media and Democracy.* Cambridge: Polity.

Kurtz, Howard. 1993. *Media Circus: The Trouble with America's Newspapers.* New York: Random House.

Lamartine, Alphonse de. 1964. In Marshall McLuhan. *Understanding Media.* New York: McGraw-Hill.

Lasswell, Harold D. 1948. In Lyman Bryson, ed. *The Communication of Ideas.* New York: Harper & Row.

Le Bon, Gustave. 1895/1960. *The Crowd.* New York: Viking Press.

Le Play, Pierre Guillaume Frédéric. 1982. *Frederic Le Play on Family, Work, and Social Change*, ed. Catherine Bodard Silver. Chicago: University of Chicago Press.

Leonard, Thomas C. 1995. *News for All: America's Coming-of-Age with the Press.* New York: Oxford University Press.

Lippmann, Walter. 1922. *Public Opinion.* New York: Free Press.

Luhmann, Niklas. 2000. *The Reality of the Mass Media.* Stanford, CA: Stanford University Press.

Marcuse, Herbert. 1964. *One-Dimensional Man: Studies in the Ideology of Advanced Industrial Society.* Boston: Beacon Press.

Marx, Karl. 1842/2001. In Hanno Hardt, ed. *Social Theories of the Press: Constituents of Communication Research, 1840s to 1920s.* Lanham, MD: Rowman & Littlefield.

Marx, Karl. 1846/1947. *Karl Marx and Frederick Engels: The German Ideology,* ed. C. J. Arthur. New York: International Publishers.

McChesney, Robert W. 1993. *Telecommunications, Mass Media, and Democracy: The Battle for the Control of U.S. Broadcasting, 1928–1935.* New York: Oxford University Press.

McLuhan, Marshall. 1964. *Understanding Media: The Extensions of Man.* New York: McGraw-Hill.

Merton, Robert. 1957. *Social Theory and Social Structure.* New York: Free Press.

Mills, C. Wright. 1963. *The Collected Essays of C. Wright Mills,* ed. Irving Louis Horowitz. New York: Oxford University Press.

Park, Robert E. 1938/1972. *The Crowd and the Public and other Essays,* ed. Henry Elsner Jr. Chicago: University of Chicago Press.

Peirce, Charles S. 1934. *The Collected Papers of Charles Sanders Peirce,* ed. Charles Hartshorn and Paul Weiss, vol. 5. Cambridge, MA: Harvard University Press.

Prakke, Henk. 1968. *Kommunikation der Gesellschaft.* Münster: Regensberg.

Pynchon, Thomas. 1973. *Gravity's Rainbow.* New York: Viking.

Redfield, Robert. 1953. *The Primitive World and its Transformations.* Ithaca, NY: Cornell University Press.

Royce, Josiah. 1913. *The Problem of Christianity.* New York: Macmillan.

Schiller, Herbert I. 1971. *Mass Communications and American Empire.* Boston: Beacon Books.

Schramm, Wilbur 1965. In id., ed. *The Process and Effects of Mass Communication.* Urbana: University of Illinois Press.

Schudson, Michael. 1978. *Discovering the News: A Social History of American Newspapers.* New York: Basic Books.

Shils, Edward. 1959. In Norman Jacobs, ed. *Culture for the Millions.* Boston: Beacon Press.

Sinclair, Upton. 1919. *The Brass Check: A Study of American Journalism.* Pasadena, CA: published by author.

Smith, Adam. 1776/1976. *An Inquiry into the Nature and Causes of the Wealth of Nations.* Chicago: University of Chicago Press.

Smythe, Dallas. 1994. In Thomas Guback, ed. *Counterclockwise: Perspectives on Communication.* Boulder, CO: Westview.

Stieler Kaspar. 1695/1969. *Zeitungs Lust und Nutz.* Bremen: Schünemann.

Sumner, W. Graham. 1934. In W. Graham Sumner and Albert G. Keller. *The Science of Society.* New Haven: Yale University Press.

Tarde, Gabriel. 1898/1969. *Gabriel Tarde on Communication and Social Influence,* ed. Terry N. Clark. Chicago: University of Chicago Press.

Thompson, E. P. 1966. *The Making of the English Working Class.* New York: Vintage.

Tönnies, Ferdinand. 1921/2000. *Ferdinand Tönnies on Public Opinion: Selections and Analyses,* ed. Hanno Hardt and Slavko Splichal. Lanham, MD: Rowman & Littlefield.

Tunstall, Jeremy. 1977. *The Media Are American: Anglo-American Media in the World.* London: Constable.

Weber, Max. 1904–5/1958. *The Protestant Ethic and the Spirit of Capitalism.* New York: Scribner's.

White, William Allen. 1924. *The Editor and his People.* New York: Macmillan.

Whitman, Walt. 1935. *Specimen Days, Democratic Vistas, and Other Prose.* Garden City, NY: Doubleday, Doran & Co.

Williams, Raymond. 1958. *Culture and Society. 1780–1950.* London: Chatto & Windus.

Winthrop, John. 1963. In Perry Miller and Thomas H. Johnson, eds. *The Puritans.* New York: Harper and Row.

Zinn, Howard. 1980. *The People's History of the United States.* New York: Harper & Row.

2 Mass Communication and the Meaning of Self in Society

Anders, Günter. 1961. *Die Antiquiertheit des Menschen. Die Seele im Zeitalter der Zweiten Industriellen Revolution.* Munich: Beck.

Bakhtin, Mikhail. 1981. *The Dialogic Imagination: Four Essays.* Austin: University of Texas Press.

Bazin, André. 1967–71. *What Is Cinema?* Berkeley: University of California Press.

Cherry, Colin. 1978. *On Human Communication: A Review, a Survey, and a Criticism.* Cambridge, MA: MIT Press.

Bibliography

Dewey, John. 1916. *Democracy and Education: An Introduction to the Philosophy of Education.* New York: Macmillan.

Einstein, Albert. 1987. *The Collected Papers of Albert Einstein*, ed. John Stachel. Princeton: Princeton University Press.

Ewen, Stuart. 1988. *All-Consuming Images: The Politics of Style in Contemporary Culture.* New York: Basic Books.

Flaubert, Gustave. 1980. *The Letters of Gustave Flaubert, 1830–1857*, ed. Francis Steegmuller. Cambridge, MA: Harvard University Press.

Foucault, Michel. 1976. *The Archeology of Knowledge.* New York: Harper.

Foucault, Michel. 1978. *The History of Sexuality I: An Introduction.* New York: Pantheon.

Freud, Sigmund. 1923/1961. *The Ego and the Id.* New York: Norton.

Fromm, Erich. 1955. *The Sane Society.* New York: Holt, Rinehart & Winston.

Godard, Jean-Luc. 1998. In Bernard F. Dick. *Anatomy of Film.* New York: St. Martin's Press.

Gouldner, Alvin. 1976. *The Dialectic of Ideology and Technology: The Origins, Grammar, and Future of Ideology.* New York: Seabury Press.

Habermas, Jürgen. 1996. *Between Facts and Norms: Contributions to a Discourse Theory of Law and Democracy.* Cambridge, MA: MIT Press.

Hall, Stuart. 1979. In James Curran, Michael Gurevitch, and Janet Woollacott, eds. *Mass Communication and Society.* Beverly Hills, CA: Sage.

Heidegger, Martin. 1927/1962. *Being and Time.* New York: Harper & Row.

Hovland, Carl. 1953. In Carl Hovland et al. *Communication and Persuasion.* New Haven, CT: Yale University Press.

Hutchins, Robert. 1967. In Floyd W. Matson and Ashley Montagu, eds. *The Human Dialogue: Perspectives on Communication.* New York: Free Press.

Innis, Harold. 1950/1972. *Empire and Communication.* Toronto: University of Toronto Press.

Joyce, James. 1916/1934. *Ulysses.* New York: Random House.

Klapper, Joseph. 1960. *The Effects of Mass Communication.* New York: Free Press.

Lacan, Jacques. 1977. *Four Fundamental Concepts of Psychoanalysis.* New York: Norton.

Lasswell, Harold. 1927. *Propaganda Technique in the World War.* New York: Peter Smith.

Lazarsfeld, Paul. 1941. In *Studies in Philosophy and Social Science*, 9:1, 2–16.

Lippmann, Walter. 1922. *Public Opinion.* New York: Free Press.

Lowenthal, Leo. 1944. In Paul F. Lazarsfeld and Frank N. Stanton, eds. *Radio Research, 1942–43.* New York: Duell, Sloan & Pierce.

Lowenthal, Leo. 1967. In Floyd W. Matson and Ashley Montagu, eds. *The Human Dialogue: Perspectives on Communication.* New York: Free Press.

Lyotard, Jean-François. 1984. *The Postmodern Condition: A Report on Knowledge.* Minneapolis: University of Minnesota Press.

Mead, George Herbert. 1934. In Charles W. Morris, ed. *George Herbert Mead: Mind, Self and Society.* Chicago: University of Chicago Press.

Niebuhr, Reinhold. 1932. *Moral Man and Immoral Society.* New York: Scribner's.

Peirce, Charles S. 1934. *The Collected Papers of Charles Sanders Peirce,* ed. Charles Hartshorn and Paul Weiss, vol. 5. Cambridge, MA: Harvard University Press.

Riesman, David. 1950. In David Riesman with Nathan Glazer and Reuel Denney. *The Lonely Crowd: A Study of the Changing American Character.* New Haven: Yale University Press.

Schudson, Michael. 1978. *Discovering the News: A Social History of American Newspapers.* New York: Basic Books.

Seldes, Gilbert. 1951. *The Great Audience.* New York: Viking Press.

Simmel, Georg. 1904/1971. In Donald N. Levine, ed. *Georg Simmel on Individuality and Social Form.* Chicago: University of Chicago Press.

Stephenson, Neil. 1992. *Snow Crash.* New Rok: Doubleday.

Talbott, William Henry Fox. 1844/1980. In Alan Trachtenberg, ed. *Classic Essays in Photography.* New Haven: Leete's Island Books.

Tocqueville, Alexis de. 1835/1966. *Democracy in America.* New York: Harper & Row.

Williams, Raymond. 1958. *Culture and Society, 1780–1950.* London: Chatto & Windus.

Wittgenstein, Ludwig. 1922. *Tractatus Logico-Philosophicus.* London: Routledge & Kegan Paul.

Subject Index

public sphere 6, 31, 32, 45, 68, 77, 82,
    107, 123, 129, 130, 136, 139

race 102, 104, 107, 116
radio 10, 36, 39, 43, 46, 55, 61, 75,
    77, 82, 83, 85, 93, 114, 123
reader(s) 10, 15, 32, 37, 39, 41, 77, 78,
    126, 133
reality 1–4, 6, 7, 9–11, 13, 24, 25, 27,
    29, 33, 43, 46, 56, 57, 63–5, 68,
    69, 83, 84, 90–2, 94, 97–9,
    101–3, 105, 107, 108, 110–12,
    115–17, 120, 122–4, 126, 127,
    130–2, 137, 138–41
religion 19, 21, 42, 59, 100, 105
reporting 9, 42, 98, 112
    see also journalism; press
representation 3, 11, 25, 44, 48, 62,
    69, 90, 92, 100, 106, 107, 120,
    122, 123, 126, 127, 140
reproduction 11, 23, 93, 107, 111, 127
responsibility 5, 38, 49, 50, 52, 69, 76,
    80, 86, 100, 108, 121, 130, 134

science 7, 33, 65, 67, 85, 93
self 6, 7, 11, 40, 84, 90, 106, 108, 109,
    110, 111, 120, 135, 138, 139, 140
social science(s) 15, 59, 63, 64, 67, 70
socialism 12, 53
sound 10, 11, 28, 94, 105
space(s) 10, 18, 20, 42, 62, 72, 80,
    108, 115, 116–20, 134, 140
spectacle 10, 11, 48, 57, 103, 110,
    139, 141
speech 4, 5, 13, 92, 126, 139
speed 18, 61–3, 100, 116, 118, 119,
    128, 130, 139
subjectivity 108, 112, 116, 119, 121,
    128, 132

taste 34, 36, 80, 83, 88, 135
    see also under culture
technology 9, 10, 14, 15, 18–20, 31,
    46, 60, 65, 75, 79–81, 85, 91, 93,
    108, 116, 118
telegraph 7, 40, 59, 118
television 5, 9, 10, 36, 42, 43, 46, 51,
    53, 55, 56, 61, 62, 72, 73, 75, 77,
    79, 83, 84, 86, 88, 93, 95, 96, 98,
    101, 102, 104–8, 112–19, 122,
    123, 125, 127, 128, 131, 132,
    133, 138
totalitarian 6, 12, 13, 88
tradition 4, 5, 39, 40, 41, 44, 60, 67,
    69, 70, 99, 110
truth 6, 23, 24, 26, 27, 42, 43, 56,
    65, 69, 79, 92, 112, 117–18, 137,
    139

United States 11, 22, 34–6, 40–2, 46,
    48, 54, 60, 62, 65, 70–2, 74, 75,
    77, 80, 82, 88, 95, 102
urbanization 11, 31, 39, 40, 41, 58, 60

viewer, the 15, 132, 133
violence 65, 72, 73, 84, 95, 101, 132
visual, the 10, 11, 16, 24–6, 36, 42,
    72, 106, 108, 110, 115, 117, 120,
    122, 124, 125, 128

wealth 25, 48, 91, 107, 135
welfare 75, 91
World War I 22, 60
World War II 15, 22, 53, 71, 80, 87,
    96
worker(s) 21, 30, 35, 47, 50, 52, 78
working class, *see* class
writer(s), writing 19, 20, 37, 39, 40,
    48, 49, 77, 78, 79, 86, 94